CW00819742

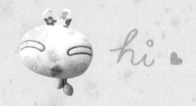

FASHION MARKET II
Interviews with 13 UK artists/designers from the fashion market
王怡穎 Yi-Ying Wang

玩心大發

I still enjoy going to markets.
Endless creative thoughts and souls increase as days go by.
The London market scene is ever so exciting and inspiring and
my reasons for going are still the same, the only difference is that
I have met so many friends through writing this book and the last one.
These friends are a great inspiration to me and going to the market has
become an even more meaningful activity because of them!
The Spitalfield's Market has gone through a major change while
I have been documenting this second book and half of the market
has closed due to the construction of a big new shopping complex.
No one knows the market's future and this is a continuing worry.

The nearby Old Truman Brewery's "Up" Market has gradually
and quietly become established and has certainly injected a new blood
into the London market scene and has lifted the spirits of the area.

Some traders have transferred from the Spitalfield's Market to the "Up" Market.
It's low rent has also been an attraction for younger designers and artists to
launch their creative businesses and to express their thoughts and ideas.
They make it a less commercial place -
a place full of real creativeness and originalities.

In this book I have gathered together people from both markets,
some have been market traders for a long time, some are new-comers
and some have become established well enough to leave the market,
but they all have the same attitude - that of trying to make a living whilst
maintaining their dreams and being true to themselves.

We all agree that it is not easy to be an artist or designer.
Sometimes you just need to follow what your heart tells you,
be a little bit more adventurous and consistent, just like everyone
who has contributed to this book and I thank them all for their time and effort.

Hope this book will bring your inner child out -
be playful, realise your dream and act on your imagination.

我仍然很喜歡逛市集，

創意百出、想法新鮮的設計師、藝術家有增無減，

倫敦市集景象依然活潑，

走在其中依然備受啟發。

去市集的心情沒變，

唯一不同的是因為發表創意市集而交了許多朋友，

每回來到市集總是話題不斷，

好像自己也融入成為其中一分子。

在記錄這第二本《創意市集》的同時，

Spitalfield's Market 也走入轉型期──

大型新商場的建設方案迫使 Spitalfield's Market 將一半的區域關閉。

正當大家憂心於她未來走向的同時，

在轉角五分鐘路程的老啤酒廠中，

卻悄悄地興起了另一個 UP Market⋯⋯

為倫敦市集打了一劑強心針。

UP Market 中，有從 Spitalfield's Market 移轉陣地重闢戰場的人；

低廉的租金，也吸引了更年輕一輩的創作者進駐──

他們毫無忌諱地用作品來表現想法，

使得 UP Market 少了某種程度的商業氣息，

卻多了活力和特色十足的原創力。

在這裡我結合了 Spitalfield's Market 和 UP Market 中的人，

舊有的，新來的，

這一群人的共同點不外乎是在現實生活壓力中維持真我，

尋求能讓他們繼續盡情把玩創意的平衡點。

相信你我都同意，以創意和設計維生不容易，

而他們比別人多的是身體力行的勇氣和執著。

希望 這本書中的人物與訪談能激發你的玩心，

開始將想像力付諸實行！

FASHION MARKET II

Interviews with 13 UK artists/designers from the fashion market

王怡穎 Yi-Ying Wang

玩心大發

Spitalfield's Market

http://www.visitspitalfields.com

Spitalfield's Market，這個我稱為創意市集的地方，超過300個攤位。歷史悠久，從她周圍新舊建築的交錯中就可回溯。自西元 1666 年倫敦大火之後這裡就一直是個市集集中地，交易熱絡不絕。每天都會開放攤位供人使用，可是只有星期天才會吸引大批攤位和人潮。

在這裡，應有盡有，新鮮蔬果、古董、自製食品、服飾、家飾、唱片，和各式各樣新興設計師、藝術家的創意作品。

目前 Spitalfield's Market 的擴建計劃正在進行中，完工後將成為一個綜合性商場。

Espresso Cappuccino Caffè Latte Caffè Mocha

THE DAILY GRIND

Tel./Fax
020 7247 2418

Sandwiches Ciabatta Baguettes Panini Focaccia

the square pie company

square pie

WELCOME TO
**OLD
SPITALFIELDS
MARKET**

Remember

YOU ARE THE FUTURE of Old
Spitalfields Market – without
your support, the market
wouldn't be the thriving, exciting
and vibrant community it is
today. We hope you continue to
support the market throughout
the building work. Thank you!

Remember

YOU ARE THE FUTURE of Old
Spitalfields Market – without
your support, the market
wouldn't be the thriving, exciting
and vibrant community it is
today. We hope you continue to
support the market throughout
the building work. Thank you!

2004年開幕的
Up Market，
位在東倫敦的
The Old Truman
Brewery 老啤酒
廠中。

Up Market

The Old Truman Brewery 的建築自1995 年被重新發掘啟用，開始被多元化地運用——主要以設計和藝術活動為主，被做為時尚商展用地、學生畢業展、藝術展覽，etc.⋯⋯

Up Market 每個禮拜天營業，氣氛新鮮活潑，距離 Spitalfield's Market 和 Brick Lane 都只有 3-5 分鐘路程。

整個倫敦東區已在這幾年發展為最 in 的地區，大大小小的 Pub、Cafe、shop 和 gallery 林立，成為時髦年輕人、藝術工作者流連聚會的最佳去處。

http://www.trumanbrewery.com

SUNDAY
(UP)MARKET
FASHION / ART / LIFESTYLE / FOOD / ACCESSORIES
020 7770 6100

020

SPECIFIC FLAVOUR
Gabriela Gonzalez Larsson & Johan Krantz

www.specificflavour.com
info@specificflavour.com
sell at Sunday (Up) Market
studio address_15 Herbert Road, London E12 6AY
+44 (0) 20 8478 6807

左：Gabriela ・右：Johan

Violet 的不同面貌

從小我就很容易被長著大頭的卡通或玩具吸引，說不出什麼原因，一直到現在都是如此；所以我設計出來的卡通人物頭的比例通常都比較大，而我收集的玩具更是可以組織大頭兵團。有此癖好的我很自然的在逛 Up Market 時，第一時間就注意到原創力十足的 Violet——一個隨著情緒好壞而將自己偽裝成不同角色的大頭小傢伙。

Violet 的創作者是一名瑞典和西班牙混血女生 Gabriela，大眼長髮，有著安靜的氣質（實際上和她活潑的個性有點出入）。她的男朋友 Johan，戴著黑色粗框眼鏡，略蒼白，也是一股安靜的氣質（他真的是滿安靜的）。他們相識於一個瑞典北邊小鎮的漫畫學校，五年前一起來到倫敦就讀大學；2004 年底二人合創了 Specific Flavour 品牌，將他們的漫畫卡通創作，以網版印刷的方式呈現在不同的產品上，例如椅墊、菜瓜布、圍裙、Ｔ恤、包包、枕頭套、日曆卡片等，應有盡有。目前的產品主角以 Violet 為主，它圓圓的大頭，像一朵朵音符，跳躍在他們 100% 手工製造的產品上，使他們的市集攤子顯得活潑鮮明。

說到 Violet 的故事和個性，Gabriela 表示 Violet 簡直就是她情緒的投射。當她開心時，Violet 會變成一個友善純真的小甜甜；當她覺得生活有點悶時，Violet 又會偽裝成專門在你睡覺時把你的夢偷走的小怪獸。「Violet 的特性就是它會不斷地偽裝成不同的身份，出其不意的出現在你身邊。」我很喜歡傾聽 Gabriela 說話，看似文靜的她談起創作過程時，那股熱切想表達自己的急躁和認真很容易讓人跟她一起興奮起來。

Gabriela 和 Johan 都愛極了畫漫畫，時時都在找尋創作來源。也許在一堆人裡他們顯得安靜害羞，不善於表達自己，可是一旦進入屬於他們自己的想像空間，會發現他們的想法有如萬花筒般隨心所欲變化無窮。兩人皆屬崇尚自然派的年輕人，一起租了個兩房一廳，附帶小花園的房子，在小花園裡他們親手種起蔬果，身體力行健康新飲食觀。兩人年紀輕輕就有一致的共識——期待幾年以後回到他們出生的家鄉瑞典，回復自然、不喧嘩的生活，走向更隨心的創作方向……

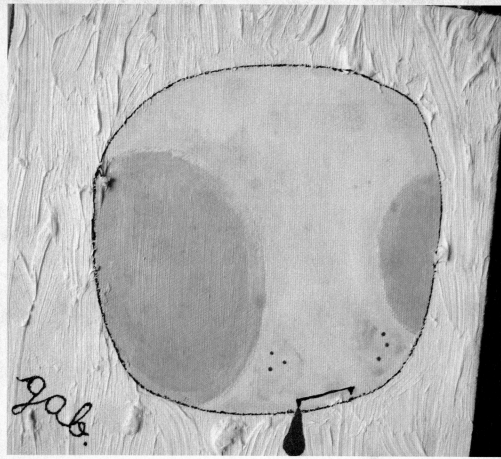

Gabriela 的畫作

＊·跟大家談談 SPECIFIC FLAVOUR 吧！你們是如何想
　　出名稱及產品概念的？
　　SPECIFIC FLAVOUR 這個名字反應出我們對於
　　沒有主張盲目追隨潮流的不認同，並為擁有不同
　　的品味偏好喝采；我們認為沒有所謂的「好」或
　　「不好」，只有「特殊品味」，所以我們應該慶
　　祝各種不同品味的相容並存，而不是阻擾其發展
　　空間。我們的作品就是針對特殊品味的人而設計
　　的特殊品牌……沒錯！

＊·透過 SPECIFIC FLAVOUR，你們想表達些什麼？
　　我們並沒有特別想藉由這個品牌去表達些什麼，
　　因為我們的作品很隨性。他們就像深入我們想法
　　的窺視孔，讓那些對我們有興趣的人一探究竟。

＊·你們是如何把這個品牌打入市場的？
　　SPECIFIC FLAVOUR 大約在一年前透過一系列
　　不同的展覽而開始出現，如 Hidden Art Fair [1]、
　　Made in Clerkenwell [2] 及 East London Design
　　Show 等，展出一系列色彩鮮豔、由塑膠回收物
　　所製成的環保配件。在那之後，我們設計出我們
　　的品牌主角 Violet，並且在 Designfront 04 設計
　　展中推出它的處女秀，該設計展主要是展出倫敦
　　藝術家及設計師的室內與時尚作品。

1　倫敦時尚市場之一，每回展覽均在戶外公開販售超過 200 位
　　主要設計師與創作者的作品，範圍從傢俱到流行時尚不等。
2　倫敦克拉肯渥綠色協會主辦的戶外物流市場。

Tell us a bit about SPECIFIC FLAVOUR. How did you come up with the name and concept?

The name SPECIFIC FLAVOUR mirrors our look on trends as something 'for the weak and feeble' and stands as a celebration of different tastes emphasising that there is no 'good' nor 'bad', only specific taste and we should celebrate the diversity of taste instead of suffocating it. Therefore we are a SPECIFIC FLAVOUR to suit a specific taste...yep.

What are you expressing through SPECIFIC FLAVOUR?

We don't particularly plan what to express with SPECIFIC FLAVOUR as our work is pretty spontaneous. We just see our work as little peepholes into our minds which we'd like to share with the people who are interested.

How did you launch the brand onto the market?

Specific flavour launched about a year ago with a series of shows, such as The Hidden Art Fair, Made in Clerkenwell and the East London Design Show where we showed our selection of colourful, recycled accessories made from plastic packaging.
Our character Violet was born a little bit after that and was first shown at Designfront04, a show including interior and fashion based work by British based artists and designers.

Please introduce yourself & tell us about your background.

We are two nature sick youngsters surrounded by concrete and asphalt. We are not really aliens but not really humans. Our ways crossed when we studied comics in a small village in northern Sweden and we have been inseparable ever since. We have different backgrounds, Gabriela in fine art based work such as painting and sculpture and Johan in film and photography. We moved to London in 2000 and since then Gabriela has completed a degree in Art & Design at Central Saint Martins College of Arts and Design and Johan has done a course in animation and is now studying photography at the London College of Printing.

How did you first become aware of and become interested in design?

First and foremost we see ourselves as artists. Design is something that we have become aware of when attempting to create usable things out of our art in order to make it available to 'the common man'.

＊· 請簡單介紹一下自己並跟大家説説你們的背景。
我們是兩個愛好自然，但卻被困在鋼筋和柏油之中的年輕人，我們不是外星人，卻也不像人類。我們相遇在瑞典北部一個小村莊的漫畫課程，自此形影不離。我們來自不同的背景：Gabriela 主修繪畫和雕塑，Johan 則主修電影和攝影。2000年一起搬到倫敦，Gabriela 在倫敦中央聖馬丁藝術設計學院 (Central Saint Martins College of Arts and Design) 完成藝術設計學位，Johan 學過動畫，目前在倫敦印刷學院 **3** 主修攝影。

＊· 你們是怎麼開始注意到設計領域並對它產生興趣的？
基本上我們一直視自己為藝術家，會去注意到設計是因為我們試著要把作品變成有用 / 能用的東西，好讓一般人可以擁有。

3 London College of Printing，2004年改名為倫敦傳播學院 (London College of Communication)。

可愛的產品吊牌

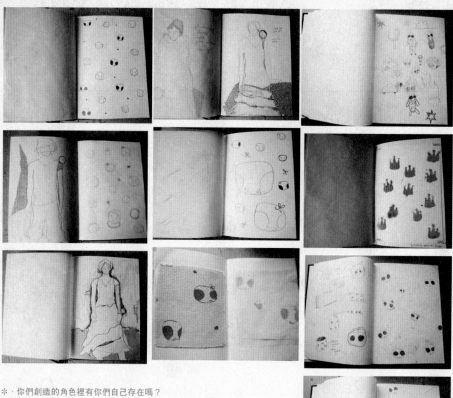

Gabriela 的隨手塗鴉本

＊．你們創造的角色裡有你們自己存在嗎？
我們相信我們做的任何事都有某部份的自己存在
其中，像 Violet 就有個和 Johan 一樣的鼻子。

＊．你們如何描述你們的設計風格？
非常富故事性。

＊．你們的產品有哪些種類？
我們什麼產品都有，從室內裝潢、時尚配件、一
直到純藝術作品，還有動畫及平面媒體等。

＊．請描述一下你們的工作程序。
目前我們做很多網版及攝影圖像印刷的工作，對
我們來說不斷更新自己是很重要的一件事。由於
我們的工作性質觸及不同領域，也因此經常調整
工作方式。

＊．你們如何推銷並販賣你們的產品？
除了 Up Market 之外，我們也透過不定期舉辦的
商品秀及展覽來推銷我們的藝術作品，同時我們
也在建立自己的網站，好讓顧客們線上消費以及
得知我們的最新消息。

＊．你們對 SPECIFIC FLAVOUR 的目標及期望為何？
期望能在 2008 年攻佔大部分歐洲市場，並在
2015 年征服世界。在那之後我們希望太空旅行
的價錢能變得便宜些。哈哈哈哈！

＊．從你們開始這個品牌作業以來，讓你們感到最開心的
事情是什麼？最難過的呢？
最開心的──做自己的老闆。
最難過的──也是做自己的老闆。

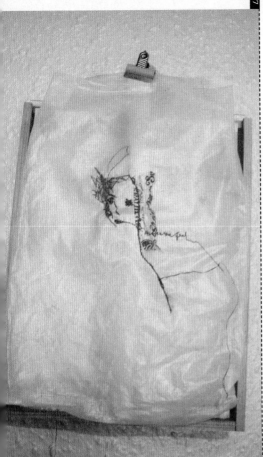

Is there a part of you in the characters you created?
We believe there is a part of us in everything we do.
Violet has definitely got Johan's nose.

How would you describe your style of design?
Full of stories.

What product range do you have?
We make everything from interior and fashion
accessories to fine art objects and projects including
animation and book based media.

Please describe your working procedure.
At the moment we work a lot with silk screen and
photographic print. It is important for us to renew
ourselves constantly. We run a cross-disciplinary
practice and because of that we're always revising our
way of working.

How do you promote and sell your products?
Apart from Up Market we promote and sell our artwork
through contemporary shows and exhibitions.
We're also in the midst of setting up a website where
we will have an online shop and lots of info.

**What's your vision and mission for SPECIFIC
FLAVOUR?**
We're hoping to take over the major part of Europe
by 2008 and by 2015, the world. After that we're
hoping that space travel has become cheap enough
ha!ha!ha!haaa!!

**Since you started your brand, what has been the
joyful thing that has happened to you? And the
most difficult?**
Joyful: Being our own bosses.
Difficult : Once again being our own bosses.

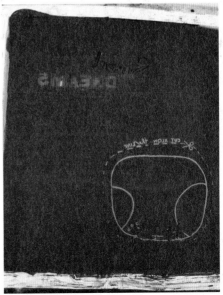

印刷網版

工作室

＊・你們有任何其它工作嗎？
我們也是自由插畫家。

＊・你們會不會從以前或當代的其他創作者身上得到靈
感？
Jhonen Vasquez [4]、Dinosaur Jr. 樂團、Chris
Ware [5]、Jean-Pierre Jeunet [6] 及 Marc Caro [7]，
等。

4　美國著名漫畫家，風格以黑色及血腥為主。
5　美國地下漫畫家。
6　著名導演，台灣熟知的作品為《艾蜜莉的異想世界》。
7　著名導演，1995 年曾與 Jeunet 共同執導《黑店狂想曲》。

＊・你們最喜歡的品牌或人物（可以是任何領域的）以及
理由？
Spooky，會吱吱叫的小玩意兒，Jhonen
Vasquex 設計的玩偶。喜歡它是因為它會吱吱
叫！

＊・如果不做設計這行你們會從事什麼工作？
不知道耶，我們有在設計嗎？也許我們會變成每
天把手指插入土裡的園丁，或是在顯微鏡下尋找
小怪獸，也許努力賺錢，環遊世界。誰知道呢？

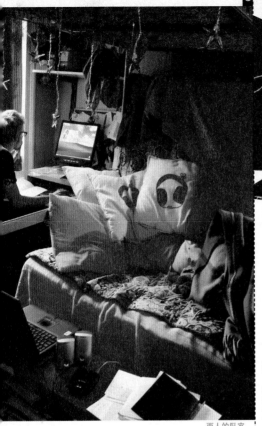

兩人的臥室

產品吊牌

Do you have other job?
We also do freelance illustration.

Do you draw inspiration from the work of other creators - historic or contemporary?
Jhonen Vasquez, Dinosaur Jr, Chris Ware, Jean-Pierre Jeunet and Marc Caro.

Your favourite brand or character (can be in any category) and the reason.
Spooky, 'the thing that squeaks', created by Jhonen Vasquez. Because it squeaks!

What would you be doing if you weren't designing?
Dunno, are we designing? Maybe poking with our fingers in the soil, looking at tiny monsters through a microscope, earning money, travelling the world, who knows?

What other forms of business would you like to venture into one day?
A commercial organic, vegan kitchen garden somewhere in the country or maybe in the middle of a metropolis selling only weird vegetables, like round carrots, polka dot stripy beetroots and maybe also homemade tea.

What's a typical day like for you?
Waking up (in case we haven't been up all night) deciding: coffee or tea? Looking for that spark of inspiration, finding it (hopefully) creative, or just do boring administrative work that no one wants to hear about.

＊・你們還會想要挑戰哪一種行業呢？
商業有機培育蔬果，在鄉村某個地方弄個有機蔬菜栽培園，或者在市中心賣些奇奇怪怪的蔬菜，像圓形的胡蘿蔔、充滿圓圓斑點和條紋的甜菜根和自己種的茶葉吧。

＊・請跟大家描述你們的一天。
起床（在我們沒有熬夜的情況下），想著：要喝茶還是咖啡？尋找靈感、（希望）發現它很有創意，或者只是做做你們也不會想聽我說的無聊行政工作。

 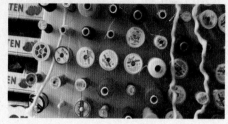

＊ ‧ 一星期中你們最喜愛哪一天？理由為何？
星期天晚上，那是唯一我們可以坐下來休息，喝杯酒的懶人時光。

＊ ‧ 一星期中你們最討厭哪一天？理由為何？
不知道是哪一天。反正我們很討厭它！

＊ ‧ 你們都怎麼打發時間？
看一堆電影，聽 Caesars Palace 的專輯，弄得一團亂！

＊ ‧ 你們奉如聖典的東西是什麼？
寬頻，嗯⋯⋯

＊ ‧ 你們此刻讀些什麼書？書的內容是什麼？
這個嘛，我們倆最近（不是同時）都讀了保羅‧奧斯特 (Paul Auster) 的《紐約三部曲》(New York Trilogy)，我們不想破壞氣氛跟大家講結局如何，不過這是保羅‧奧斯特寫的書。它的其中一篇故事〈玻璃城市〉（"City of Glass"）已被改編成繪本，很好看。

＊ ‧ 你們最喜愛和最討厭倫敦哪一點？
喜愛——我們的花園、外賣店、多樣性、博物館、國家公園、酒吧、鸚鵡、雙層巴士。
討厭——無禮、冷淡、自私、麥當勞、星巴克、咖啡共和國、Costa 咖啡連鎖店、吐痰、便溺、地鐵中央線、地鐵北線、交通。天啊！我們在這幹麼啊？

＊ ‧ 當工作或思考遇到瓶頸時你們都怎麼做？
尖叫。

＊ ‧ 你們如何應付壓力？
尖叫。

＊ ‧ 你們現在過的是夢想中的生活嗎？如果不是，你們夢想中的生活型態和地點為何？
不是，不完全是。我們的想法經常在改變，目前夢想中的生活型態是住在瑞典海邊的老舊別莊，在那裡安靜地做我們的藝術創作。

＊ ‧ 讓你們維持生活步調及常規的事物是什麼？
咖啡和肉桂興奮劑，以及在夜晚聽音樂。

＊ ‧ 你們最喜歡的飲料、音樂類型和電影是什麼？
飲料：不含乳品的飲料。音樂：目前我們聽的任何音樂（現階段是 The Concretes 樂團、Tom Waits 及挪威 Burzum 樂團）。電影：Gummo。

＊ ‧ 怎麼樣會特別討你們開心？
大太陽底下，坐在我們花園裡快要解體的長板凳上喝杯冰啤酒。

What is your favourite day of the week? And why?
Sunday evening. That's the only real lazy time we get
Sit's when we kick back with a bottle of wine.

What is your least favourite day of the week? And why?
We don't know which one it is. Anyway we hate it!

What do you do to kill time?
Watch a lot of films, listen to Caesars Palace and make a hell of a mess.

What's your bible?
Broadband, eerm...

What book are you reading at the moment? And what's it about?
Well, we both recently read (not at the same time) *New York Trilogy* by Paul Auster. We don't want to spoil the ending, but it's written by Paul Auster. Anyway, one of the parts City of Glass, has also become a graphic novel, which is also a good read.

What do you love and hate the most about London?
Love : Our garden, takeaways, diversity, museums, lee valley nature reserve, pubs, parakeets, routemasters
Hate : The rudeness, carelessness, selfishness, mcdonalds, starbucks, coffee republic, costa, spit, shit, piss, central line, northern line, traffics, god, what are we doing here?

What do you do when you are stuck on a particular design/idea?
Scream.

How do you handle your stress?
Scream.

Are you living your ideal lifestyle right now? If not, what's your ideal lifestyle & place to be?
No, not really. It changes all the time, but at the moment our ideal lifestyle would be in a worn out cottage by the sea in Sweden, where we can make our art in peace.

What keeps you going and stay in tune?
Coffee and cinnamon caffeine pills, late night music.

What's your favourite drink, music & film?
Drink: Non-dairy smoothies.
Music: Whatever we're listening to at the moment (now The Concretes, Tom Waits and Burzum).
Film: *Gummo.*

What would be a special treat for you?
A cool beer in the hot sunshine on the fall apart pallet bench in our garden.

產品包裝紙

以 Violet 為主角的系列產品

＊・你們通常都怎麼烹調馬鈴薯？
　　這不是我們平時烹調馬鈴薯的方法，但它比
　　較有趣。在我們瑞典有個很棒的馬鈴薯品種
　　Ohasselbackspotatis，將它洗淨、削皮、切成薄
　　片，但不要切到底部，如此才能維持形狀不變。
　　放在烤盤上，灑些油、大蒜和麵包屑，再放進烤
　　箱裡烤。

＊・夢想中的工作是？
　　差不多就是我們現在所做的，但要能達到一般倫
　　敦市民的收入標準。

＊・什麼是你們從有嘗試過、但有一天一定會去做的一
　　件事？
　　印刷在 Brunswick Centre 大樓上（這是位於倫敦
　　Bloomsbury 區的一幢灰色、非常立體派又能激
　　發人靈感的混凝土大樓）。

＊・最近迷些什麼東西？
　　藍莓、紅莓、香蕉混合的綜合水果飲料。

＊・什麼是你們生活中不可或缺的？
　　誠實，咖啡機，音樂。

＊・請用簡短的一句話來描述你們自己。
　　Gabriela　頑固的小混蛋。
　　Johan　戴著眼鏡的無恥小人。

＊・要不要跟大家分享你們的祕密？
　　前陣子我們挖走附近草原上的一株黑莓樹。我們
　　相信這就叫偷竊。

＊・夢想能……
　　變成書呆子。

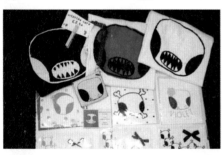

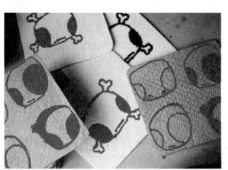

What's your usual way of cooking potato?
This is not our usual way but it's more interesting.
There is something really good in Sweden called
'hasselbackspotatis' (trans. Hazel Hill potato).
Wash and peel the potatoes, cut thin slices into them
leaving the bottom part untouched so they keep their
shape. Put them on a ovenproof dish and sprinkle some
oil, garlic and breadcrumbs on the top and shove them
in the oven.

A dream job to you is...
About what we do right now, but with the normal
salary of a standard London citizen.

**What have you not tried to do, but would definitely
want to try one day?**
Screen print over Brunswick Centre (a very grey, cubist,
inspiring concrete block in Bloomsbury, London).

What's your latest obsession?
Blueberry-raspberry-banana smoothies.

What can't you live without?
Honesty, coffee maker, music.

Please describe yourself in a short sentence.
Gabriela   Stubborn little bastard.
Johan   Cheeky bastard with glasses.

Dare to share one of your secrets?
The other day we dug up a blackberry bush from the
meadows near where we live. We believe this is called
stealing.

Dream to be?
A nerd.

20th CENTURY ICONS

Matthew Thatcher

www.monkeyink.co.uk
matt@monkeyink.co.uk
sell at Sunday (Up) Market
studio address_74 Worton Road, Isleworth, Middlesex, TW7 6HG

左：Matt；中：Ann；右：女兒 Amelia

"Imagination is more important than knowledge."

einstein

"There is only one difference between a madman and me—the madman thinks he is sane.. I know I am mad."

marley

marley

lone wolf & cub

laurel & hardy

michael

-dean

mr. white

zola

gauguin

bruce

dali

picasso

sammi

rolf

van gogh

geronimo

warhol

marilyn

einstein

hitchcock

20TH CENTURY ICONS 的不同人物滑鼠墊

一張愛因斯坦伸出舌頭的卡通畫像，吸引我走近 Matt 位在 Up Market 的攤位。這是一張我們都再熟悉不過的照片，但設計者用幾條簡單的線條就抓住了愛因斯坦調皮的神韻，旁邊配上他說過的話："Imagination is more important than knowledge."（想像力比知識更重要）。圖畫簡潔，卻生動有張力。再看看其他圖畫，全是我認識或不認識的名人卡通畫像配上他們的名言。這些名言的篩選都別具用心，搭配活潑的卡通肖像，呈現出詼諧、聰明的整體幽默，看了引人會心一笑。我站著瀏覽了一下，攤位的主人 Matt 緩緩向我過來，高高瘦瘦的他，用溫和的語調，友善地跟我打招呼並且開始解說他的作品。

Matt 長得很像他自己畫筆下的梵谷，很多人都曾問那是不是他的自畫像。他不說話時給人一種距離感，或者說是一種威嚴，可是當他說起他的作品來可是滿腔自信，淘淘不絕。沒有受過正統的美術教育，Matt 畫畫完全是憑著一股熱情無師自通。從小他就是大家眼中那個「無時無刻都拿著筆的小孩」，六歲開始喜歡畫人，畫電視上的人、畫家人、畫卡通漫畫裡的人。三十年之後，Matt 喜歡畫人的那股熱忱仍未曾減退。廣泛閱讀書籍的他，開始畫他仰慕的人或對他有影響力的人。

20TH CENTURY ICONS 的概念來自於他讀到畢卡索的一席話（請參看訪談內容），這席話當下帶給他無法言喻的驚喜，讓他非得用畫筆把它們記錄下來不可。沒想到一畫不可收拾，從此畫名人及他們的名言變成 Matt 生活中重要的一部分。Matt 說他想畫的人太多，這些人帶給他不同的靈感和生活中的啟發，而透徹地了解不同名人的故事，幫助他更準確地抓住他所想要表達的感覺和感情，也更能確切詮釋他畫筆下人物的神韻。

週一到週五在看板設計公司任職的 Matt 和另一半 Ann 以及寶貝小女兒 Amelia 住在倫敦西南距離西斯羅 (Heathrow) 機場不遠的地方。他們養了一隻貓咪和一隻變色龍蟋蜴，Matt 平常畫畫的工作室則是由家中的車庫改造而成。畫畫一直只是他個人的興趣，直到開始在 Up Market 銷售他的 20TH CENTURY ICONS 系列之後，才又帶給他另一股不同的動力。他直率的提到因為多了別人對他作品的肯定，現在的他對畫圖除了喜愛，又多了一分認真。以前很少會完整的完成一幅畫，現在則不斷地從完成的畫作中得到成就感，覺得生命更喜悅。

Matt 是一個認真的人，不論對畫圖，對家庭，還是對中國民族功夫的鑽研（這點真的把我嚇了一大跳，對此他還真的是下了功夫去研究，而且還有未來計畫，請看訪談內容），讓我看到了尚未成名的藝術家的堅持與執著。

Matt 的卡通漫畫

* · 跟我們談談你的工作與藝術作品。你是怎麼想出 20TH CENTURY ICONS 的整體概念的？

其實這整個概念一直都存在我腦海中，但我想真正的催化劑應該是讀了畢卡索的一段引言之後：「我母親曾對我說：『如果你想從軍，你終將成為一名將領；如果你想做一名修士，你終將成為教宗。』但我只是成為了一名畫家——畢卡索。」對我而言，這段話意味深遠到我必須將它與畢卡索的肖像結合，畫在一起。但畫完之後，他看來是那麼孤單，所以我又畫了梵谷和達利，同樣的也配上他們說過的名言。之後就沒有停止過這樣的創作，因為有太多讓我景仰同時又希望將他入畫的人！

從小我就常畫朋友和家人的卡通和肖像漫畫，我也會在任何筆能沾到的地方作畫。記得有一次跟家人去渡假，因為身邊沒有素描本子，我還畫在衛生紙上。（衛生紙很難畫，因為它一下子就破了。）

在學校時我總是把課本畫得亂七八糟的，經常被教訓，但卻又無法抑制我的藝術衝動。每星期一開始時我總是會有包好的嶄新課本封面，然後到了星期五的時候又得重新再換新的封面。

* · 透過你的藝術作品你想表達些什麼？

透過 20TH CENTURY ICONS 我想表達出這些名人平時不為人知的一面。我會在作品上透過一句慎選的引言為他們增添一份獨特的性格。希望觀看者能由這些肖像畫看到這些名人迄今不為人知的個性，並且在某種程度上與他們結合在一起。

* · 請自我介紹並跟大家說說你的背景。

這個嘛，我叫 Matthew Thatcher，今年三十六歲，跟我的搭檔 Ann 住在倫敦西南區，育有一名二十個月大的女兒 Amelia。我的嗜好和消遣是武術、爬山、健行和露營、閱讀、下廚、和三五好友及家人相聚及收藏舊日本武士刀！

我從學校畢業後立即投入社會行列，第一份工作是網版印刷技術員，自此換了很多有趣的工作。我做過裱框者、印刷員和自由設計師，現在從事招牌看板業。

很遺憾的是我為了要賺更多錢買我想要的東西而放棄追求更高學歷。所以學校畢業後我開始做全職工作，為我自己買了部福斯金龜車，並且把每一分賺來的錢都花掉！

幾年後我試過要上大學（在我賣掉我的車後），並且在倫敦動畫學院 (London Cartoon College) 註冊。那是個短期課程，教你如何畫卡通。然而我覺得自己水平高出他們太多，因為我自己從小就一直在做這些課程表中的練習，所以課還沒結束我就開溜了。後來我又註冊學習電腦 3D CAD（Computer Aided Design）課程，但這次我更急，走得更快！

Tell us about your works & art. How did you come up with the 20th CENTURY ICONS concept?

The concept has pretty much always been at the back of mind.

But I guess the catalyst to the 20th CENTURY ICONS was from reading a great quote by Picasso.
My Mother said to me Oif you become a soldier you'll end up as a general. If you become a monk you'll end up as the Pope. Instead I became a painter and wound up as Picasso. This to me was just so expressive I had to incorporate it with his caricature. But he looked so alone, so along came paintings of Van Gogh and Dali, again with these great quotes I had found and I haven't stopped since. They're just too many interesting icons that I admire and wish to paint!

From a young age I've always drawn cartoons and caricatures of friends and family, I would draw on anything that a pen would stick too, I remember one occasion, whilst on holiday, I used toilet tissue to draw on because I didn't have my sketch book. (Toilet tissue is useless to draw on it rips so easily!)

Whilst at school I would doodle over my books, getting into trouble and unable to control my artistic urges. I would start out with a freshly covered book on Monday and having to recover it again by Friday!

What are you expressing through your works?

With the 20th CENTURY ICONS, I try to express a version of these people in a way that hasn't been seen before! I'll add a unique personality to the painting through a carefully chosen quotation. Hopefully the viewer might see a side to the icon's personality hitherto unknown and connect with them on some level.

Please introduce yourself & tell us about your background.

Well, my name is Matt Thatcher and I am 36 years old, I live in South-West London with my partner Ann and we have a 20 month-old daughter Amelia. My hobbies and pastimes are Martial Art, climbing, hiking and caving, reading, cooking, having fun with my friends and family and collecting old Japanese swords!

I started working straight after leaving school as a silkscreen printer and had many interesting jobs along the way. I've been a picture framer, printer, and freelance designer and am currently working in the sign industry.

Much to my regret, I decided to forgo further education in favour of having the money to buy things I wanted! So upon leaving school I started full time work and bought a VW Beetle, and spent every penny I earned on it!

I did attempt to go to College a few years later (after I had sold my car) and enrolled in the London Cartoon College. It was a short course on how to draw cartoons. However, I felt a little over qualified, as I had pretty much covered most of the syllabus myself anyway. I left without finishing and enrolled on CAD course and rather rashly, I left that one early too!

＊‧你是怎麼開始注意到藝術並且對它產生興趣的？
小時候每個人都很有創造力，在著色簿、素描本子和牆上瘋狂塗鴉！有些孩子隨著年紀的增長愈來愈少畫畫，將注意力放在別的事情上。等到他們成人後你會聽到他們說：「我真希望自己會畫畫！」

我的腦袋總是放在素描本或漫畫書上，我孩提時最早的靈感該是來自於一部叫《舊金山街道》(The Streets of San Francisco) 的影集，美國七〇年代的警匪劇。裡頭的主角 Karl Malden 擁有我童年時期所看過最巨大的鼻子！那鼻子讓我印象深刻到我必須把它畫下來才行！我該謝謝他才對，因為他讓我後來對肖像漫畫如此鍾愛。

＊‧你選擇作為筆下主角的標準是什麼？
由欣賞、崇拜他們為出發點。我有一大串感興趣的、很棒的人物名單，他們都擁有某些我想抓住的特質。

＊‧你最喜歡自己的哪一個作品？理由為何？
常常會變，但此刻我想我個人最喜歡的是愛因斯坦肖像。我很喜歡畫他的感覺，和他旁邊的那句話：「想像力比知識更重要」——那似乎給了他一個全新的性格。

很奇怪，但卻是事實的事情是：2003 年，亞伯‧愛因斯坦曾孫的乾媽來參加了我的第一個肖像展，她為愛因斯坦的曾孫買下了那幅肖像！

＊‧你如何描述你的藝術風格？
流行卡通的形式！用智慧的筆觸畫出簡潔明亮的風格！

＊‧請描述你工作的程序。
我會先盡我所能找到一堆我要畫的人物的照片，然後輕描速寫地畫、直到我對他們的樣子感到滿意為止。然後再用電腦掃描成為線條構圖，必要時會為他們上色。接著就是我最愛的、為他們尋找適當引言的時間，結合這些語錄能讓我的肖像畫活起來！

＊‧你如何推銷並販賣你的產品？
我有個網站：www.monkeyink .co.uk。目前在 Up Market 有個攤位，很快地會在倫敦 Greenwich Market 開設另一個攤位。

我一直很幸運，透過人們不斷的推薦，讓我的工作機會一直不斷。

＊‧你對 20TH CENTURY ICONS 的期望及目標為何？
我有個能讓整個空間亮起來、既特別又有原創性的點子，哈哈！沒啦，說實在的，我非常喜愛現在的肖像畫系列，目前並沒有放棄這個部份、改走另一個藝術領域的打算。

最近我在擬定一個可以在今年夏天讓英國各商店及藝廊推銷並販賣我作品的計畫。總而言之，讓我作品的曝光率更高！

＊‧從你開始這個品牌作業以來，最讓你感到開心的一件事是什麼？最難過的呢？
大眾給予我作品的正面評價讓人不可置信，非常感謝他們給我的所有迴響。在他們瀏覽我作品時聽聽他們的想法是很有趣的一件事，如果能聽到他們的笑聲那就更棒了！

How did you first become aware of and become interested in art?

As children, we are all so creative to begin with, we love to draw, and we scribble madly in colouring books, sketchpads and walls! Some children spend less and less time with their art as they grow up and more time on other things. Once they've grown up, you'll hear them say as adults, I wish I could draw!

I always had my head in either a sketchbook or a comic book! But my very earliest inspiration as a child came from watching an episode of *The Streets of San Francisco*, an American 70's police drama. One of the actors Karl Malden had the biggest nose I had ever seen in all my young years! It made such an impression on me that I just had to draw It! I Can thank him for my lifelong passion for caricature art!

What's your criterion on choosing characters to paint?

I admire them for starters. I have a huge list of fantastic people I wish to paint! There is something in their personalities I wish to capture.

Which one of your works is your favourite? And why?

It does change occasionally, but I would say that Einstein is my personal favourite at the moment. I had great fun with him and the quote 'Imagination is more important than knowledge' seems to give another level of character to him.

※ · 你有任何其它工作嗎？

有的，我在倫敦西區一間展覽及劇場招牌公司擔任全職的經理工作。

※ · 藝術家是很難掌握的一個工作嗎？身為一位藝術家，感覺如何？

一點也不！我想不出其它更好的工作了，它的各層面我都很喜歡。我天生的創意對我而言是很重要的一部分。我的藝術需要一個輸出管道，即便到最後只是在浪費油彩畫一幅畫，也沒有關係，因為我已經從環繞我四周的世界偷走了一點時間到我的工作室中。

※ · 你會從以前或同時期的一些藝術家作品上找靈感嗎？

我很欣賞某些藝術家。像我真的很喜歡莫迪里亞尼 (Amedco Modigliani) 近乎印象派肖像畫風、梵谷厚重的顏料及高更的大地風。我喜歡霍奇金 (Howard Hodgkin) 的抽象畫、夏卡爾 (Marc Chagall) 夢幻般的畫、畢卡索扭曲的畫風及克林姆 (Gustav Klimt) 分離的拼湊油畫風格。

小時候，Rolf Harris 對我來說跟神一樣，他在幾分鐘之內完成的十公尺長油畫，簡直超出我信仰的境界了！

Strange but true fact: The first exhibition of Icon paintings in 2003 was attended by Albert Einstein's Great Grandson's Godmother Kathi Lindisbacher! She bought the painting for him!

How would you describe your style of art?

It's a kind of cartoon pop! Bold and bright with a touch of wisdom!

Please describe your working procedure.

It starts with trying to find as many photos as I can of the subject to paint. I will then loosely sketch them until I'm quite happy with the look, I'll scan it as a line art and then colour them as necessary. The thoroughly enjoyable aspect of choosing appropriate quotes comes next, which when incorporated with the caricature brings it to life!

How do you promote and sell your works?

I have a website: www.monkeyink.co.uk.

I currently have a stand at Up Market and will shortly be opening another at Greenwich Market, London.
I have been quite lucky to receive a lot of work through recommendation too.

What's your vision and mission for 20th CENTURY ICONS?

I have a unique and original concept that can brighten up a dull room ha-ha! No seriously, I am thoroughly enjoying myself with the Icon series and have no plans to stop and go in another artistic direction just yet.

Currently, I'm setting out a structure to promote and sell my work in shops and galleries throughout the UK this summer. In a nutshell, I want to have my work seen by as many people as possible!

What has been the most joyful thing that has happened to you since you started the 20th CENTURY ICONS? And the most difficult?

The positive response from the general public has been incredible, I'm grateful for all the feedback I've had from them! Its fun to listen to their comments as they browse my works and when I hear laughter it makes it perfect!

Do you have any other job?

Yes, I have a full time job as a manager, for an exhibition and theatre signage company in West London.

Is being an artist difficult job to handle? How are you feeling being one?

No not at all! I couldn't think of anything better, I really enjoy every aspect. The creative side of my nature is a deeply important part of me. My art needs to have an outlet, even if I just end up wasting paint on a canvas, it doesn't matter to me so much as I have taken some time away from the world around me to escape to my studio.

Do you draw inspiration from the work of other artists - historic or contemporary?

There are several artists I admire. I really like the almost-caricature style of Modigiliani. Van Gogh's fantastic thick impasto, the earthiness of Gauguin.
I love Howard Hodgkin's abstracts and Chagall's dreamy scenes. Picasso's twisted forms and the gilt patchwork quilt paintings of Klimt.

As a child Rolf Harris was like a god to me, his incredible 10m long paintings finished within minutes were beyond belief!

Matt 的車庫工作室

✳ · 你最喜歡的品牌或人物（可以是任何領域的）是什麼？理由為何？

我沒有特別喜歡的品牌，但以人物來說，我最喜歡黑澤明導演導的某部片中的演員三船敏郎，他是個優秀的日本演員，飾演周旋在黑白兩道之間一個既卑鄙又可悲的角色，他的演出有種近乎動物的野性。黑澤明高深的說故事功力總是能在駭人的劍術對決、幽默感及戲劇張力間取得平衡點。

✳ · 如果不是做這行你會從事什麼工作？

也許會對自己說：「噢！真希望我會畫畫！」

✳ · 你還會想要挑戰哪一種行業呢？

我希望能為兒童建造一些特別的育兒室和房間，替他們畫壁畫，給孩子們一個又亮又酷又有趣的天地！接著我希望在五年內能開一間學校，教授中國武術詠春拳的基礎。

✳ · 請試著描述你的一天。

一般來說都挺累人的，我通常早上六點半起床，然後馬不停蹄地工作直到晚上十一點半就寢為止。我女兒大多會在我手忙腳亂東碰西撞準備上班時醒來，所以我們在我出門前可以有一小段時間相處。早上八點到下午五點我在招牌公司的產品製作部門擔任經理工作，工作時間長短不一，交貨期間會忙昏頭，不過很值得。

夜晚則總是在我試圖要填滿它時飛快流逝，我會致力於我的新點子直到眼皮快闔上為止。極少情況下我會無所事事，若是那樣，就表示我蠟燭兩頭燒得沒力了，身心都需要放個假！

✳ · 對你來說，全世界最能激發你靈感的東西是什麼？

我的女兒 Amelia！我創作過的最完美的作品！

✳ · 一星期中你最喜歡哪一天？為什麼？

以前來說會是星期五，因為那表示在工作了一個星期後我可以有兩天假期！但現在來說是星期天，因為那天我會到市集去，認識一堆有趣的人並跟他們交談真是非常有價值的一件事，那一天

簡直過得太快了！星期日市集像極了一個小型家庭社區！

✳ · 一星期中你最討厭的一天呢？為什麼？

星期五——信不信由你！我永遠不知道能不能準時交貨！星期五是招牌業在一星期中最忙碌的一天。

✳ · 你都怎麼打發時間？

我是個狂熱的讀者，只要一有時間我就會渾然忘我地埋首書堆中！

✳ · 你的聖典是什麼？

一本收集了中國武術詠春拳大師黃淳樑和其他大師剪報的老舊資料夾！1950 年代黃大師曾在超級詠春大師葉問在香港的武術學苑中指導過李小龍。這些報導對於詠春拳的原理及科學依據有特別角度的介紹，即使我讀過很多次，它們還是能激發我的靈感！

✳ · 你最近在讀些什麼書？書的內容為何？

我在讀 Timothy Mo 的 The Monkey King，一本描述一個雖窮卻饒富機智的男人如何被安排入贅至一個看似優渥家庭的小說。有趣的地方在於他必須在這個吹毛求疵的大家族中運用他的機智，最後爬到眾人仰賴的地位。

✳ · 你最喜愛和最討厭倫敦哪一點？

如果你是指倫敦本身，那麼我喜歡它的博物館、歷史、藝廊、各式各樣的餐廳和商店。我不太喜歡阻塞的交通和車輛進入市中心的收費。[1]

我住在倫敦郊區，離市中心約十公里的地方，我不喜歡住在空中交通要道下在早上五點鐘傳來的飛機聲！

1 自2003年2月起，週一至週五車進入倫敦市中心皆要付 congestion charge，目前是每天五鎊。這個措施是為了紓緩倫敦市中心的車流量。

Matt 的車庫工作室

murals and making them bright, cool and fun places for kids! Secondly, within the next five years I aim to open a school, passing on the principles of the Chinese Martial Art Ving Tsun.

What's a typical day like for you?

Normally pretty hectic, I start my day at 6.30am, and I'll be on the go till I go to bed around 11.30pm.
My daughter normally wakes as I fumble around knocking into things getting ready for work so we'll spend a little time together before I leave. During the day I work 8.00 - 5.00pm at the sign company managing the production dept. The hours can be unpredictable and the deadlines are demanding but it can be very rewarding.

The evenings will generally fly by as I try to cram as much as possible into them. I'll work on new ideas till my eyelids start to droop. On those rare occasions when I just do nothing it means I have burnt the candle at both ends and my mind and body need a short holiday!

What is the most inspiring thing in the world for you?

My daughter Amelia! The most perfect piece of art I have ever had a hand in creating!!

What is your favourite day of the week? And why?

Well it always used to be Friday simply because I knew that I would have two days off after finishing work! But now it has to be Sunday because that is the day I go to the market. It's incredibly rewarding to meet and talk to so many interesting people. The day goes far too quickly! The market is very much like a little family community!

What is your least favourite day of the week? And why?

Friday believe it or not! I never quite know whether I will finish work on time! Friday's are the busiest time of week for us in the sign industry.

What do you do to kill time?

I'm an avid reader. I'll normally have my head in a book lost in the pages, if I have some moments free!

What's your bible?

It's a beaten up old clip-folder with a collection of articles on the Chinese art of Ving Tsun Kung Fu by Master Wong Shun Leung and others! Master Wong was Bruce Lee's foremost teacher at Grandmaster Yip Man's school in Hong Kong in the 50's. The articles are unique insights into the principles and science of the Ving Tsun system. Even though I've read it many times it's totally inspirational to me!

What book are you reading at the moment? And what's it about?

I'm reading *the Monkey King* by Timothy Mo. A novel about a poor but resourceful man and his arranged marriage into a seemingly wealthy Chinese family. It's very funny in a soft way as he is forced to use his wits to climb the strict family pecking order to become indispensable to them.

Your favourite brand or character. (can be in any category) and the reason?

I don't really have a preferred brand as such but my favourite character would be the Akira Kurosawa Osamurai with no name films starring Toshiro Mifune, a Japanese actor of outstanding skill. Playing a shambling, bedraggled character who runs rings around the corrupt officials and local gangs, Mifune's enigmatic screen presence is almost animal. Kurosawa's great storytelling combines thrilling swordplay black humour and gripping tension equally.

What would you be doing if you weren't painting?

Probably be saying to myself 'I wish I could draw!'.

What other forms of business would you like to venture into one day?

I like to see myself offering my services constructing unique children's nurseries and bedrooms, painting

What do you love and hate the most about London?

If you mean London itself, then I love its museums and history, the galleries, it's varied restaurants and shops the hustle and bustle. I'm not so keen on the traffic jams and congestion charges. I live in the suburbs of London, about 10km from town and dislike being under the Airport flight-path at 5 am!

Matt 在 Up Market 的攤位上

* · 工作或思考遇到瓶頸時，你都會怎麼做？

我會先休息，第二天早上精神飽滿時再來看一遍！有時候這個程序會花上三個星期，我想我必須得換個方法了。哈哈！

* · 你如何應付你的壓力？

當情況變得不可預期地糟糕時，我會試著不受影響。我可以在有潛在壓力的環境中放得很輕鬆。如果情況和場合把我惹毛時，我會試著做些氣功或詠春拳，它們能立刻轉移我的注意力！

* · 你現在過的是你夢想中的生活嗎？如果不是，你夢想中的生活型態及地點為何？

還不算！我們計畫搬到倫敦西南郊的 Cornwall 郡，因為鄉下地方總是安靜舒適。我們會有間典型的英式房屋和日式的花園和茶室！我會帶我的柴犬到我位於 St. Ives 的藝廊工作室去，賣掉一堆作品，然後傍晚回家跟家人朋友渡過晚間快樂時光，並且照顧我們養的雞！

* · 讓你維持生活步調及常規的事物是什麼？

每天迫不及待想回家接受我女兒的甜蜜笑臉和擁抱。那是最棒的一件事！

* · 你最喜歡的飲料、音樂類型及電影各是什麼？

我最喜歡的飲料是綠茶！我不是個能喝酒的人，但我的櫃子中有瓶朋友送我的苦艾酒，我計畫哪一天我要在晚上喝得酩酊大醉之後畫畫，看看我發酒瘋後會搞成什麼樣子！我那朋友也是在有一天我跟他提到有幾個大師在喝醉後出名作，才送我那瓶酒的。挺值得嘗試的呢！

我最喜歡的音樂類型啊？嗯……任何節奏較強烈的音樂都喜歡，真的！不過每個星期都會變啦！我工作時總是聽古典樂，因為沒有歌詞的音樂能讓我工作效率比較高。此刻我最喜歡的樂團是 Presidents of the USA，他們是三個懂得把有趣又瘋狂的歌詞和曲子結合在一起的怪人！像 Kings of Leon、Franz Ferdinand 樂團那一類的。

好啦，我最喜歡的電影？又是一個難題！太多了，但如果我只能選一部帶去荒島度日，我會選李小龍主演的《精武門》。我唸書時我媽媽在錄影帶店兼差，其中一項福利就是可以免費看片。我數不清媽媽把這部片帶回來給我看的次數！因為太多次了，後來錄影帶店老闆乾脆把這部片送給我，反正它也從不在架上！

What do you do when you are stuck on a particular piece of work/idea?

I'll take a break from it and look at again the next morning with fresh eyes! Sometimes its taken three weeks with this method, I need to find a new one ha-ha!

How do you handle your stress?

I try not to get wound up when circumstances unexpectedly change for the worse, I can sort of hover above some things that are potentially stressful!
If on occasion, situations do irritate me I will try some breathing and Chi Kung exercises or practice Ving Tsun, which can quite quickly refocus you!

Are you living your ideal lifestyle right now? If not, what's your ideal lifestyle & place to be?

Not quite yet! We plan to move to Cornwall in the South West of England for the relative peace of the countryside. We would have a typical English cottage but with a Japanese garden and teahouse! I would go to my Gallery/Studio in St. Ives with my Shiba Inu dog and sell lots of paintings returning home in the evening to have fun with my family and friends and tend our chickens!

What keeps you going and stay in tune?

I can't wait to get home to a big smile and hug from my daughter; it is the best thing ever!

What's your favourite drink, music & film?

My favourite drink is green tea! I'm not that much of a drinker! However I do have a bottle of absinthe a friend gave me sitting in the cupboard, I plan someday to get quite drunk on it one evening, paint, and see what sort of drunken mess I come up with! He gave me the bottle after I mentioned to him once that quite a few famous painters used to get wrecked on the stuff and went on to paint masterpieces! It's worth a shot!

My favourite music? Hmmm anything with a dirty riff really! Mind it does seem to change from week to week! If I'm working then I will always listen to classical music, I work much more effectively to music without lyrics! One of my favourite bands at the moment is the Presidents of the USA. There a quirky three piece who really know how to write fun, crazy lyrics matched up to fun and crazy music! The Kings of Leon, Franz Ferdinand that sort of thing.

Right, my favourite film? That's another tough question! So many? It's hard to choose but if I had to take one film only to a desert island it would just have to be Fist of Fury starring Bruce Lee! My mother had a part time job in a video store when I was at school and one of the perks of the job was free video. I lost count of the amount of times that my Mum bought it home for me to watch! So much so that the owner of the store ended up giving it to me as it was never on his shelf!

＊‧怎麼樣會特別討你開心？
　　我很容易滿足，任何簡單小動作的表示，往往就
　　是你當下最希望得到的東西。

＊‧你平時都怎麼烹調馬鈴薯？
　　我沒有一定的方法，總是試著交替做。此刻我喜
　　歡的烹調方法是先煮熟，再用大蒜油快炒！我也
　　喜歡老式的烘焙馬鈴薯，想迅速解決一餐沒有比
　　它更好的了。

＊‧夢想中的工作是？
　　做自己的老闆，早上能晚一個小時起床，然後在
　　工作室工作一整天後回家跟家人共度快樂時光。

＊‧什麼是你從沒嘗試過、但哪一天一定會去做的事？
　　高空跳傘、非洲探險、創作一本兒童繪本，還
　　有，放個長長的無聊渡輪假期好重新充電！

＊・你最近迷些什麼東西？
自孩提時期以來，除了藝術之外，我最沉迷的興趣就是武術了。在接觸詠春拳之前我曾鑽研過中國拳擊、空手道、劍道、太極和短棍。我可以談論武術談上幾個小時，然後輕易地讓人們覺得無聊透頂，我確定！

然而，最近迷上 eBay！它很容易讓人完全上癮，並且掏錢買些你根本不需要的東西，因為太便宜了！

同時，我也在學瑞典話。

＊・你生活中不可或缺的東西為何？
空氣。哈哈！

＊・請用簡單的一句話形容你自己。
M.A.T.T.——魯鈍的 (Moronic)、有藝術細胞的 (Arty)、頂尖的 (Top)、沒什麼用的 (Turkey)。

＊・要不要跟大家分享你的祕密？
我有個姑姑叫瑪格莉特・柴契爾。

＊・夢想能……
人們需要我時我總是會在。

What would be a special treat for you?
I'm easily bought; the simplest gesture is often the nicest thing you could wish for at the time.

What's your usual way of cooking potato?
Well I don't really have a usual way; I try to mix it up a little! At the moment, I do like them boiled first, then sauteed in garlic oil! Good old baked potato too, can1t be beaten for a quick meal.

A dream job to you is...
To be my own boss and getting up for work in the morning an hour later. Then having some fun with my family followed by a long day in the Studio.

What have you not tried to do, but would definitely want to try one day?
A parachute jump. An African safari, write and illustrate a children's book. Also to take a long boring cruise to totally recharge my batteries!

What is your latest obsession?
My unwavering obsession since a child apart from art has been Martial arts. I've studied Chinese boxing, Karate, Kendo, Tai Chi and Short Staff before settling with Ving Tsun Kung Fu. I can happily talk for hours about the Martial Arts and quite easily bore most people within minutes, I'm sure!
However, my latest obsession I would say is eBay! Totally addictive and thoroughly easy to buy stuff you don't really need because it's so cheap!

I'm also trying to learn Swedish!

What can't you live without?
Air! Ha-ha.

Please describe yourself in a short sentence.
M.A.T.T. Moronic. Arty. Top. Turkey.

Dare to share one of your secrets?
I have an aunt called Margaret Thatcher.

Dream to be...
Always there when needed.

Spoon

Naomi Avsec

www.spoonbynaomiavsec.com
naomiavsec@hotmail.com
sell at Sunday (Up) Market
studio address_22, Dunton House, Leigham Avenue, London SW16 2TN
+44 (0) 79 5648 1213

Naomi 工作室／房間一角

看 Naomi 用縫紉機畫圖看到入神……移動的技巧像鋼琴家彈琴般的流暢，運轉之間又帶有書法家任意揮灑毛筆的隨興，熟練的程度幾乎不加思索就可以在短短的時間內繡出一幅圖畫。我就像看到魔法般興奮的問她是如何辦到的？需不需要花很長的時間練習？她說從17歲學紡織設計課程就開始用縫紉機，對她而言，用縫紉機就像拿筆畫圖那麼自然，容易。紡織設計課程學到一半，Naomi 決定轉系唸插畫，如果要她定位自己，她會毫不思考地說：「畫家，或藝術家。」

瀏覽過她的畫作，我終於被她的作品說服為什麼她如此自信的定義自己，更瞭解為了什麼她不加思索就可以在短短的時間內用縫紉機繡出不同圖案、人物的疑惑。因為，她是一位充滿想像力的畫家，她的畫，天真，詭異，黑暗，夢境，樂園……我沒有試著去問她畫的背後有什麼故事或涵意，不喜歡去解讀藝術家腦子裡的東西，因為無解，任憑個人體會吧！但可以理解的是，她用縫紉機畫圖就如同她在畫板上任意作畫的道理一樣，只是使用工具的不同而已。

畫家並不是一個可以賺錢的工作，會用縫紉機也沒什麼大不了，Naomi 體認現實，也意識到她不能浪費自己在這兩方面的天份技巧；所以去年夏天，Naomi 開始在 Up Market 設攤，將她的圖畫繡在衣服上賣，第一天就賣了 250 鎊，這是她的品牌 Spoon 的開始，一個好的開始。從那天起，每個禮拜天，她都會帶著心愛的老縫紉機在 Up Market 邊繡邊賣。很多顧客打從心裡喜歡她的作品，乾脆把家裡的枕頭套、窗簾、有的沒的都拿來請她用縫紉機在上面作畫！

回想起 Spoon 開始之前，她經歷人生的最低潮期，一段感情的結束讓她感覺一夕之間好像一無所有，創作事業也是起起落落。但是這些波折卻啟開了她生命的另一扇窗，因為她豁然的面對一切的失意，努力而且誠實面對自己，嘗試重新再找回自信。她用所有的積蓄加上貸款，買了一個國宅小公寓，先給自己一個安定溫暖的家，一個安靜的創作空間（我稱她的家是品味國宅，小小的空間被她打理得清爽舒適）。她告訴我，這將近一年來，是她內心最充實開心的一年，有了新事業帶來的安全感，讓她重新定位人生，確定新目標，她覺得自己已經準備好，期待不斷的激發新的創作，期待戀愛！

Naomi 的筆記塗鴉

＊· 跟大家談談 SPOON 吧！妳是如何想出這個名稱及
產品概念的？
我很愛湯匙，很享受性愛！我也喜歡人們用湯匙
舀湯，並且，我需要一個很容易繡在衣服後頸的
品牌名稱，所以這名稱來源其實也有某部份是以
實用做為考量的。

＊· 妳透過 SPOON 想跟大家表達些什麼？
事實上我是在表達所能引起我興趣的事物。
我是個畫家，所以許多衣服上的角色是從我的畫
作、素描及所有能激發我靈感的每件事物中得來
的，如：詩、電影、音樂及文學作品等。

＊· 請介紹一下妳自己並告訴大家妳的背景。
我是科班出身，同時是擁有實務經驗的畫家及插
畫家。過去十年我在倫敦及里茲二地的 Harvey
Nichols 百貨公司，還有格拉斯哥的 Jenners 百
貨公司都展示過畫作。

＊· 妳如何定位妳自己？（一個畫家？織品設計師？時裝
設計師或藝術家？）
我喜歡將自己歸類為藝術家和畫家，我不認為自
己是時裝設計師。感覺自己現在做的事比較像是
個人藝術領域的一種延伸，也更容易廣為大眾接
受。

Tell us a bit about SPOON. How did you come up with the name and concept?
I love spoons and I love spooning!! I also love soup which you eat with a spoon. I also needed a name that I could embroider easily onto the neck labels!! So it was partially for practical reasons.

What are you expressing through SPOON?
Basically I am expressing all that interests me. I am a painter, therefore a lot of the characters on my clothes are from my paintings, drawings and everything that inspires me e.g: poetry, film, music and literature.

Please introduce yourself & tell us about your background.
Painter and illustrator by education and trade. I have exhibited for the past ten years including showing my works at Harvey Nichols in London, Leeds and Jenners in Glasgow.

How do you position yourself? (As a painter? Textile designer? Fashion designer or artist?)
I like to think that I am an artist and painter, I don't really see myself as a fashion designer. I feel that what I do is more an extension of my art and that it is a more accessible area for the general public.

Each piece unique &
embroidered freehand
by NAOMi AVSEC
Tel: 07956 481 213
vw. spoon by naomiavsec.com
COMMISSIONS WELCOMED

Each piece unique &
embroidered freehand
NAOMi AVSEC
el: 07956 481 213
spoon by naomiavsec.com

Naomi 的居家兼工作室

＊・ 妳有沒有把某部份的自己畫在或刺繡在妳創作出的那
　　些角色中？
　　當然！在我的設計中絕對有頑皮、淘氣、莽撞的
　　一面，而這些都是我個性中的一部份。

＊・ 妳覺得自己的藝術風格是什麼？
　　另類、超現實的、肉慾的、幽默的、黑暗的、張
　　牙舞爪的、富表達性的。

＊・ 妳的產品有哪些種類？還想將觸角伸向何處？
　　Ｔ恤、運動衣、連帽運動外套、包包、裙子、領
　　帶、絲巾。

＊・ 跟大家說說妳的工作程序。
　　將衣服反過來，然後把我腦中粗略形成的想法和
　　想要繡的東西繡上。基本上我用縫紉機來繪圖。

＊・ 妳如何推銷並販賣妳的產品？
　　我目前只在市集擺攤，但希望能弄台電腦、儘快
　　將我的品牌資訊寄給各報章雜誌。

＊・ 妳對 SPOON 的期望及目標為何？
　　我希望在市集的服務範圍能擴大並且變得更受歡
　　迎。例如做更多的訂做服務（通常我會帶著我的
　　縫紉機和一堆空白的衣服去市集，我的速度很
　　快，通常客人在一頓午餐之後就可以來取貨）。
　　我也想讓某些特定的商店批發我的產品，選出幾
　　個較受歡迎的設計，然後大量製作以降低批發成
　　本。

＊・ 從妳開始這個品牌作業以來，讓妳最開心的事情是什
　　麼？最難過的呢？
　　開心的事——從我的顧客那裡得到的回應總是
　　很棒！還有 *Independent* 報紙、*Nylon* 雜誌和
　　fuk.co.com 刊登過關於我的品牌的文章。
　　難過的事——市集生意不穩定造成的財務不安全
　　感。

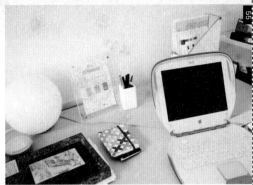

Is there a part of you in the characters you draw or embroider?
Definitely. Cheeky, mischievous, saucy elements are definitely in my designs and are a part of my character.

How would you describe your style of art?
Idiosyncratic, surreal, sensual, humorous, dark, sinister, illustrative.

What product range do you have? And to expand?
Tees, sweats, hoods, bags, skirts, ties, scarves.

Please describe your working procedure.
Interface the reverse side of the garment and then embroider freehand with a rough idea in my mind of what I want to embroider. Basically I use the machine to draw.

How do you promote and sell your products?
I only do the market at present, but hoping to get a computer and start blitzing all magazines and newspapers with my press release.

What's your vision and mission for SPOON?
I would like my service at the market to expand and become even more popular. E.g more commission work while I am there. (I take my sewing machine there and lots of blank items of clothing and offer a bespoke service while the customer goes off for their lunch etc.) And I would like to wholesale to a select few shops. Maybe even get a couple of more popular designs mass produced so that I have a cheaper range for wholesale.

Since you started your brand, what has been the most joyful thing that has happened to you? And the most difficult?
Joy - the response I get from customers about my product is always wonderful!! Also the press I had in the *Independent* and *Nylon* magazine and the story fuk.co.uk ran on my label.
Difficult - the financial insecurity from the ups and downs of market life.

Do you have any other job?
I have a textile agent (designing samples for the fashion industry) and sometimes work for a website gallery called numasters.com.

Is being an artist a difficult job to handle? How are you feeling being one?
I love most of what being an artist brings apart from the financial stresses.

Do you draw inspiration from the work of other artists or designers - historic or contemporary?
Yes of course, all the time, constantly.

＊ · 妳有別的工作嗎？
我有一個織品代理商（為時尚業者設計樣本），有時我也為一個叫 numastars.com 的網路藝廊工作。

＊ · 藝術家是很難掌握的一件事嗎？身為一位藝術家的感覺如何？
撇開財務壓力不談，我喜歡身為一名藝術家所帶來的大部份事物。

＊ · 妳會不會從過去或當代的其他藝術家或設計師身上得到靈感？
會，當然，一直都是，經常地。

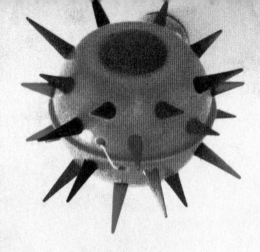

＊· 妳最喜歡的牌子或人物（可以是任何領域）以及理由？
　　奈良美智，我喜歡他作品中的色彩、情緒、以及黑暗與幽默並存的感覺。

＊· 如果不是做這行妳會從事什麼工作？
　　性工業。

＊· 妳還會想要挑戰哪一種行業呢？
　　房屋（室內設計）、傢俱設計（手工刺繡椅等）、替一些性感的時裝設計師刺繡。

＊· 跟大家描述妳的一天。
　　新鮮空氣、食物、泡澡、點蠟燭、音樂、畫畫、刺繡以及更多的刺繡、閱讀、跟朋友嬉鬧及可能看場電影。

＊· 對妳來說，全世界最能激發妳靈感的東西是什麼？
　　愛、生活、食物和性。

＊· 一星期中妳最喜愛哪一天？理由為何？
　　星期一是我的星期日（因為它是我的假日）。

＊· 一星期中妳最討厭哪一天？理由為何？
　　跳過這問題吧。

＊· 妳如何打發時間？
　　時間是寶貴的，所以我不打發它。

＊· 妳奉行不渝的守則是什麼？
　　微笑。

廚房一角

Your favourite brand or character. (Can be in any category) and the reason?
Yoshitomo Nara. I love the colours, the vibe, the darkness and the humour in equal measures.

What would you be doing if you weren't doing what you are doing now?
Sex Industry.

What other forms of business would you like to venture into one day?
Property (interiors), furniture design (embroidered chairs), embroider for some sexy fashion designers.

What is a typical day like for you?
Fresh air, food, soak in a bath, candles, music, drawing, embroidering and more embroidering, reading, laughing with friends and possibly a movie.

What is the most inspiring thing in the world for you?
Love, life, food and sex.

What is your favourite day of the week? And why?
Monday is my Sunday (because its my Sunday).

What is your least favourite day of the week? And why?
Pass.

What do you do to kill time?
Time is valuable so I don't kill it.

What's your bible?
Smile.

Naomi 的畫作

❊ · 妳此刻正在讀些什麼書？書的內容是什麼？
Adam Phillips 的 *Going Insane*，他是位心理醫師，教人如何快樂，並且持續快樂下去。

❊ · 妳最喜愛和最討厭倫敦哪一點？
我喜歡它的多樣性及生命力（新世界與舊世界並存），討厭它過多的高樓大廈及侵略性的風氣。

❊ · 當工作或思考遇到瓶頸時妳都怎麼做？
出去跑步或騎騎車。

❊ · 妳如何調適妳的壓力？
運動（瑜珈），喝杯紅酒。

❊ · 妳現在過的是妳夢想中的生活嗎？如果不是，妳夢想中的生活型態及地點為何？
蠻想住在海邊的。

❊ · 讓妳維持生活步調及常規的事物是什麼？
伏特加、紅牛活力飲料及印度拉茶拿鐵。

❊ · 妳最喜歡的飲料、音樂類型和電影是什麼？
飲料參考上題，電子音樂及所有電影。

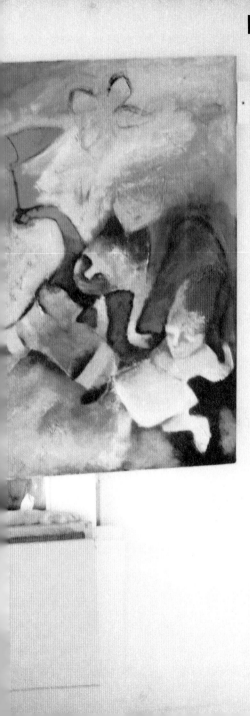

What book are you reading at the moment? And what's it about?
'Going Insane' by Adam Phillips (written by Psychoanalyst about being happy and staying there)

What do you love and hate the most about London?
I love its diversity and vibrancy (old and new together). I hate the lack of sky space and the aggressive vibe.

What do you do when you are stuck on a particular work/idea?
Go for a run or cycle.

How do you handle your stress?
Exercise (yoga) glass of red wine.

Are you living your ideal lifestyle right now? If not, what's your ideal lifestyle & place to be?
Would quite like to live near the sea.

What keeps you going and stay in tune?
Vodka and Red Bull and chai tea latte.

What's your favourite drink, music & film?
See above, eclectic music and film.

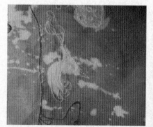

Spoon 品牌服飾

What would be a special treat for you?
Getting on a plane and visiting a new country, somewhere near the sea and sun.

What's your usual way of cooking potato?
Mashed potato.

A dream job to you is...
No money world, just 'swapped services'.

What have you not tried to do, but would definitely want to try one day?
Fly a plane or preferably a helicopter oh and ski too.

What is your latest obsession?
What I can embroider next... and men.

What can't you live without?
Friends, my sewing machine and my mitsubishi pen.

Please describe yourself in a short sentence.
Tall, curly, smiley with a lust for life and mischief.
Also extremely loyal and empathetic.

Dare to share one of your secrets?
I once slid down a firemans pole extremely drunk and tore a ligament in my ankle and ended up on crutches for 6 weeks. (My boyfriend at the time said it served me right for flirting with firemen!)

Dream to be...
Totally and utterly in love.

＊‧怎麼樣會特別討妳開心？
坐上飛機到某個靠海又有陽光的陌生國度。

＊‧妳都怎麼烹調馬鈴薯？
做成馬鈴薯泥。

＊‧夢想中的工作是？
無需用到錢的世界，只有「交換服務」。

＊‧什麼是妳從沒有嘗試過、但有一天一定會去做的一件事？
開飛機，直昇機更好，噢，還有滑雪。

＊‧最近迷些什麼東西？
我下一個要刺繡的東西……和男人。

＊‧什麼是妳生活中不可或缺的？
朋友、我的縫紉機和我的三菱牌的筆。

＊‧請用簡單的一句話來形容妳自己。
高挑、捲髮、喜歡笑，渴望生活，愛耍淘氣。同時也極度忠誠、富同情心。

＊‧要不要跟大家分享妳的祕密？
有一次我喝太醉從消防滑杆上滑下來，結果傷了腳踝韌帶，拄著枴杖六個星期。（我當時的男友說這是我跟消防隊員調情的代價！）

＊‧夢想能……
完完全全地沉浸愛河。

LIGHTS OUT

Mark Dunn

markkdunn@btinternet.com
sell at Sunday Spitalfield's Market

Mark 在 Spitalfield's Market 的攤位

Mark 和女友 Sian

在 Spitalfield's Market 後段的一個角落，總是有個攤位，掛著一盞盞設計典雅、色系溫和的吊燈與燈罩，在鬧哄哄的市集中，鵝黃的燈光靜靜散發，顯得格外寧靜有氣質。初見設計師 Mark 時，我一股無法掩飾的驚訝全部寫在臉上：有著運動員身材、外表粗壯的他，竟然設計風格和手工是如此細膩。他的個性和我想像中也不同，顯得溫和、沉穩；基本上他是那種初見時會讓人不太敢親近他，可是熟識了就會不由自主喜歡他的人。

Mark 在大學唸的是產品設計，從那時起他就對燈的結構和設計特別感興趣，畢業後朝著這個興趣發展，成為全職燈具設計師至今已十年。而已經有四年市集經驗的 Mark 總是在全職工作之餘，將時間安排得恰到好處。市集提供了他在朝九晚五的工作步調之外，自由發揮設計的機會和空間。這幾年來，由於定期在市集的曝光，讓他的作品受到注目，進而被刊登在許多英國的傢飾雜誌中，同時也陸陸續續在一些頗有名氣的店家中展售。

曾被最多雜誌介紹，也是他賣的最好的一個設計，是印有人形圖案環繞的燈，他用特殊的印刷方式將人形線條溶解，讓燈光得以藉由這些人形從其身上透射出來，活力又有個性。我自己最喜歡的則是他的復古鬍鬚吊燈——一個東西合壁感情濃厚的設計。平常 Mark 也接受客戶的特別訂做，他就曾經幫一位經營酒吧的客戶做過一盞高達一公尺的大鬍鬚吊燈。Mark 的產品價格都在 30 鎊上下，合理的價錢和精緻的品質絕對是他能在市集中生存這麼多年，而業績仍然穩固的原因。

訪問是在 Mark 和他從大學時期就開始交往的女友 Sian 二人的家中進行，Sian 同樣也從事設計工作，是一位成功的內衣設計師。他們兩著住家裝飾得溫馨有風格，Mark 的燈具懸掛在不同房間中也顯得很搭調。平常若他們兩人都得在家工作時，會各自佔兩頭不同的房間，Sian 的那間堆滿時尚雜誌和剪貼；Mark 這頭則是他的製燈工具和網版，所有的燈具從材料印刷到成品全在這間小房間內獨立製作完成。他還當場示範做了一盞燈，手法純熟，但對每個細節卻絕不馬乎。雖然只是簡單的示範製燈過程，可是 Mark 自然流露出的專注神情和重視細節的態度，我知道，他是認真的看待這個一生的事業。

Mark的作品刊登在雜誌上

* · 跟大家談談 LIGHTS OUT 吧！當初你是如何想出這
  個名稱及整個產品概念的呢？
  LIGHTS OUT 這個名詞在拳擊賽中是表示把對方
  擊倒或一擊的意思，我們通常也用這個詞來形容
  某件看起來非常棒的東西。

* · 你透過 LIGHTS OUT 想跟大家表達些什麼？
  表達我設計各式燈罩的才能。

* · 你當初是怎麼打入這個市場的？
  之前有個朋友也在市集賣東西，她總是說我也該
  來賣賣我的一些燈作，於是我就這麼開始了。開
  始賣的第一週我就賺了超過二百英鎊，這讓我蠻
  驚訝的。幾週後我發現銷量不斷增加也就繼續做
  了下去，直到現在。

* · 你當初是怎麼意識到並且開始對設計產生興趣的？
  從我大學時代的一個老師那裡。

* · 請描述你工作的程序。
  很零亂啦。

* · 你認為產品應該是以功能為主還是以外觀為主？
  我想這應該會依設計不同而有所不同吧！

* · 你打算擴大你產品的領域和種類嗎？
  我現在正在思考各種不同的概念，它們可能引導
  我往任何方向走。

* · 你如何推銷並販賣你的產品？
  透過媒體──包括 *Elle Decoration*、*Living Etc*、
  Guardian 及各國際報章雜誌等，以及寄電子郵件
  給顧客。

* · 你對 LIGHTS OUT 的期望及目標為何？
  成為街坊上的一間超酷燈店。

Tell us a bit about LIGHTS OUT. How did you come up with the name and concept?
The term lights out in boxing terms means to knock someone out or knock out. We also use the term knock out to describe something that looks great.

What are you expressing through LIGHTS OUT?
My ability to design good lampshades.

How did you launch the brand onto the market?
I had a friend that used to do the market. She always said that I should go down and sell some of my lights.

I went down and signed up, the first week I took over £200 which surprised me. The weeks after saw an increase in my sales so I kept at it up until now.

How did you first become aware of and become interested in design?
From a teacher at my college.

Please describe your working procedure.
Sporadic.

Form follows function or function follows form?
I think that this depends on what you are designing.

Are you going to expand your product to a wider range and variety?
I am looking at lots of different concepts at the moment, which could lead me in any direction.

How do you promote and sell your products?
Emails sent out to customers, press (*Elle Dec, Living Etc, National Papers - Guardian* etc.).

What's your vision and mission for LIGHTS OUT?
To become an amazing lighting store on the high street.

印刷網版

*· 你賣得最好的一項設計或產品為何？為什麼？
　以 Devore 方式印製，上有人形圖案的設計燈，
　顧客都覺得它很炫。

*· 你個人最喜愛的一項設計或產品為何？為什麼？
　蘋果電腦的 ipod，它看起來很酷。

*· 從你開始販賣燈具到現在，最讓你感到開心的一件事
　是什麼？
　顧客們喜愛、欣賞、並且花錢買下我設計的東
　西。

*· 最感到難過的呢？
　人們不喜歡我的設計。

*· 設計師是很難掌握的一個工作嗎？身為一位設計師的
　感覺如何？
　有時真的挺困難的，不過我很享受體會箇中甘
　苦。

*· 你會從過去的或當前的一些設計師作品上找靈感嗎？
　各種的設計師我都會參考。

*· 你最喜歡的品牌或人物（可以是任何領域的）是什
　麼？理由為何？
　蘋果電腦──它真是無敵酷的！

*· 你如果不做設計師你要做什麼呢？
　也許當ＤＪ吧？？？

家中走廊上掛著 Mark 做的鬍鬚吊燈

What's your best selling design/product? And why?
My Devore lights with the people design around it. Customers think that it is funky.

What's your favourite design/product? And why?
The ipod by Apple. It looks cool

Since you started your product line, what has been the most joyful thing that has happened to you?
Customers love, enjoy, and buy my designs.

And the most difficult?
People how are negative.

Is being a designer a difficult job to handle? How are you feeling being one?
Sometimes it can be difficult but I enjoy it nether the less.

Do you draw inspiration from the work of other designers - historic or contemporary?
Various designers.

Your favourite brand or character (can be in any category) and the reason?
Apple - coooooooool gadgets.

What would you be doing if you weren't designing?
DJ...???????

What other forms of business would you like to venture into one day?
To have my own restaurant.

What's a typical day like for you?
I work full time for a supplier to Laura Ashley and John Lewis (production manager/design), after work I make stock for the market. Two days a week I go to the gym. Socialise with friends on the weekends.

What is the most inspiring thing in the world for you?
My Mother.

What is your favourite day of the week? And why?
Friday because it's the end of the week.

＊· 你還會想要挑戰哪一種行業呢？
擁有我自己的餐廳。

＊· 平常你都是如何度過一天的？
我在 Laura Ashley and John Lewis 的供應商那裡擔任全職的品牌經理及設計師，下班後則做做市集中要賣的商品。一星期上兩次健身房，週末和好友聚聚。

＊· 對你來說，全世界最能激發你靈感的東西是什麼？
我的母親。

＊· 一星期中你最喜歡哪一天？為什麼？
星期五，因為它是最後一個工作日。

Mark 和 Sian 養的貓

What is your least favourite day of the week? And why?
Monday because it is the start of the week.

What do you do to kill time?
Play music.

What's your bible?
Teaching from my mother.

What book are you reading at the moment? And what's it about?
Where did you get those - Trainers/Sneakers.

What do you love and hate the most about London?
I was born and raised here and I love it and hate it.

Things I hate - traffic.

Thing I love - it's a multi-cultural city more than most other places in the world.

What do you do when you are stuck on a particular design/idea?
Go for a walk and come back and try to find more inspiration.

How do you handle your stress?
Take deep breaths. Go and visit a good friend.

Are you living your ideal lifestyle right now? If not, what's your ideal lifestyle & place to be?
I have many ideals, it is impossible to choose.

What keeps you going and stay in tune?
My girlfriend

房間的燈飾

＊‧一星期中你最討厭的一天呢？為什麼？
星期一，因為它是開工日。

＊‧你怎麼打發時間？
放音樂。

＊‧你奉行不渝的守則是？
我母親的教誨。

＊‧你最近在讀些什麼書？內容為何？
Where Did You Get Those?，有關球鞋及運動鞋的書。

＊‧你最喜愛和最討厭倫敦哪一點？
我在這裡出生長大，對它又愛又恨。討厭的地方——交通。喜歡的地方——它是個多種文化組成的城市，比其他地方豐富得多。

＊‧當設計或構思出現瓶頸時，你通常都怎麼做？
出門散步，再回來看看能否有更多靈感。

＊‧你如何應付壓力？
深呼吸、出門拜訪朋友。

＊‧你現在過的是你夢想中的生活嗎？如果不是，你夢想中的生活型態及地點為何？
我夢想太多了，很難選。

＊‧讓你維持生活步調及常規的事物是什麼？
我的女朋友。

Mark 的燈作

＊‧你最喜歡的飲料、音樂類型及電影各是什麼？
存放七年的 Havana Club [1]、嘻哈音樂、《星際
大戰第六部曲：絕地大反攻》。

＊‧怎麼樣會特別討你開心？
請我在一家昂貴的餐廳吃頓晚餐。

＊‧你平時都怎麼烹調馬鈴薯？
水煮。

＊‧你的理想工作是？
擁有我自己的連鎖燈具傢飾店。

＊‧什麼是你從沒嘗試過、但有一天一定會去做的事？
高空跳傘。

＊‧你最近都迷些什麼東西？
ＤＪ混音機（DJM 909 型號）。

＊‧你生活中不可或缺的東西為何？
音樂。

＊‧請用簡單的一句話形容你自己。
快樂、無憂無慮、好相處。

＊‧要不要跟大家分享你的祕密？
不要。

＊‧夢想能……
快樂以終老。

1 以古巴當地品質最佳的甘蔗蒸餾而成，酒味溫和、酒質透
明，通常至少要存放十八個月才能裝瓶出售。

What's your favourite drink, music & film?
7-Year Havana Club, Hip Hop, *Return of the Jedi*.

What would be a special treat for you?
Dinner at an expensive restaurant.

What's your usual way of cooking potato?
Boil it.

A dream job to you is...
To own my own chain of lighting and interior stores.

What have you not tried to do, but would definitely want to try one day?
Sky diving.

What is your latest obsession?
DJ mixer (DJM 909).

What can't you live without?
Music.

Please describe yourself in a short sentence.
Happy, care free, and easygoing.

Dare to share one of your secrets?
No.

Dream to be...
OLD AND HAPPY WTH MY LIFE.

As Twee As It Can Be

Amanda Doyle, Liz King & Sanna King

Amanda Doyle
mail@sannapanda.co.uk

Liz King
www.moretrifle.com
lizbeth_cakeeater@hotmail.com

Sanna King
www.sannapanda.co.uk
mail@sannapanda.co.uk

sell at Sunday (Up) Market.
our shop_Kingly Court, London; meet your maker - Sydney St,
Brighton; and soon to be in Motel, Covent Garden, London.
studio address_Unit 1b, 178a Glyn Road, Hackney, London, E5

左：Sanna；中：Amanda ；右：Liz

Liz 的手工卡片

Liz 的手工筆記本

你有沒有做過這樣的白日夢？和幾個好朋友合開一家小咖啡館……咖啡館就座落在一片綠意盎然的寧靜中（靠海也可以），有空一起喝喝下午茶，什麼都可以聊，店裡還兼賣一些精緻有品味的小東西（若是能自己設計最好），日子過得舒服愜意沒有一絲勉強……Amanda，Liz 和 Sanna，告訴我這個夢，而這個夢在她們的想像中越來越具體，好像走過一個轉角就快到了……

三個自然不做作的女生，一直是感情融洽的朋友，都喜歡塗鴉、織毛線、裁縫，都有一雙巧手，喜歡自己動手做東西。志同道合的她們有一天決定一起在 Up Market 租個攤位來分享她們的巧手之作。攤位總是乾淨清新，作品釋放出很女生的、恬恬淡淡的、融合在花草自然元素之中的感覺，是一個好像會散發出花香的攤位，難子每樣東西的設計和成品皆出自三人之手，有布胸針、卡片、針織小錢包、椅墊、T恤、包

包、筆記本、毛帽等等，居然連真的很好吃的漂亮小蛋糕也是 Liz 親手做的！細緻的手工和細部點綴的巧思，雅緻又可愛，不同的作品，放在一起卻有異曲同工之妙。

坐在她們身邊聽她們說話，總是很輕鬆，可能是因為她們身上都散發出自然悠閒的氣質和溫和的態度，如同她們的作品一樣。Amanda 特別喜歡打毛線，連看電視時也打，坐在市集裡也打，躺著站著都可以打，所以針織品是她的主要產品。她和 Liz 一樣，都是紡織設計師，Liz 的手工筆記本和她一針一針繡出來的圖案對話卡片總是令人愛不釋手。平常在書店工作的 Sanna 則鍾情於不同布料的收集和拼貼，用它們做出不同的包包飾品。跟她們一邊聊天時我竟然已經開始幻想她們未來的店面長的是什麼樣子，心思這麼細膩的三個女生，一定可以經營出一家讓你一走進去就不想出來的舒適品味小屋……

Liz 的手繪本

﹡‧ 跟大家談談 AS TWEE AS IT CAN BE 這個牌子。妳們是怎麼想出整個產品概念的？

Amanda 是由一個「等一會兒如果妳給我看妳作品的話，我也會給妳看看我們工作室的作品。」的對話開始的，那時我們覺得，既然有相同的目標和想法，一起合作會很不錯。後來有個朋友跟我們提到 Up Market，剩下的你們就都知道了，很老掉牙的故事！

Sanna Liz 和 Amanda 在看顧攤位時想到這個名字，好笑的是在 4 年前大學的一個童鞋專案作業中，我早就用過這個名字了。

Liz 那時我們已經在市集中擺攤了，也真的很喜歡我們攤位的樣子，所以有一天我們東想西想，覺得這攤位看起來真的很可愛，結果這個名字就這麼浮了上來。它真的超適合我們手工製的作品！

﹡‧ 請介紹一下自己並說明妳們的背景。

Amanda 我是個高個兒，利物浦約翰莫爾斯大學 (Liverpool John Moores University) 畢業，主修織品服裝，之後我到過紐約、舊金山等地，一路從事設計工作！我在許多設計工作室及童裝公司待過，現在覺得該是時間走自己的路了。

Sanna 我媽媽是芬蘭人，所以一直以來我都很喜歡斯堪地那維亞（北歐）的設計風格和手工產品，而我爸爸是藝術家，所以他們一直很支持我，沒有因為我決定主修鞋子與袋子的設計學位而生氣。

我在學校時就認識貓熊 (Amanda)，我們談論製作袋子談了好幾年，終於真的執行了！

Liz 我來自一個充滿藝術氣息的家庭，生長於一個鳥不生蛋的地方，所以我跟我姊姊會花好幾個小時用廁所滾筒衛生紙和喜瑞爾早餐紙盒做東西。我們總是在創作。

Sanna 的作品

Tell us about AS TWEE AS IT CAN BE. How did you come up with the name and concept?

Amanda After a brief 'I'll show you my work if you show me yours' in the design studio we decided it would be good to collaborate on something as we had the same ideas and goals. A little birdie told us about Up Market and the rest as they say is history!

Sanna Liz and Amanda came up with the name while sat on the stall, but funnily enough I had already used it for a children's shoe project in college 4 years ago.

Liz We had already started going to the market , and we were really pleased about the way it looked. So we were just day dreaming about it one day, thinking how it looked really cute, and I think the name just came out, and it fit our hand made, craft based look perfectly!

Please introduce yourself and tell us about your background.

Amanda I am a tall bird, who went to Liverpool John Moores Uni and completed a degree in Fashion and Textiles and flew to as far as New York and San Francisco designing along the way! I have worked for numerous design studios and childrenswear companies and felt it was time to have a go at doing my own thing.

Sanna My mum is finnish, so I've always appreciated Scandinavian design and crafts. And my dad is an artist of sorts, so they've always been really supportive, and didn't go mad at me when I decided to do a degree in shoes and bags!

I've known Panda (Amanda) since school and we've talked about making bags and stuff for the last few years and finally we've got round to it!

Liz Well I come from a very arty family. I grew up in the middle of no where so me and my sisters would spend hours making things out of toilet rolls and cereal packets. We were always creating.

What are you expressing through AS TWEE AS IT CAN BE?

Amanda I guess I feel we are almost showcasing and selling a passion and hobby that excites us all.

It's a collaboration of designs and products that we hope people enjoy and chuckle at as much as us!

Sanna It's all about unique hand-made things that make you smile or giggle.

Liz The right to create crafts for the modern girl!

How did you launch the brand onto the market?

Amanda A close friend opened a lovely little shop in Brighton and suggested we put some things in there. It just grew from that.

Sanna We starting selling a few knitted bags and corsages in a friend's shop in Brighton. They got noticed by a couple of small magazines and gemma from our shop contacted us about supplying them.

Liz We started at the Sunday Up Market, we basically had a few things laid out on a table! Sanna and Amanda had already been selling in a few shops, but it was the first time for me!

※ · 妳們透過 AS TWEE AS IT CAN BE 想表達些什麼？

Amanda 我想我們是在販賣一個不停激發著我們的熱情與嗜好。這是一個結合了設計與產品的牌子，我們希望人們會喜歡，並且能和我們一樣對這些作品發出會心一笑。

Sanna 它就是個特別的能讓你微笑甚或傻笑的手工製產品。

Liz 表達為摩登女孩設計東西的權利！

※ · 妳們如何把這個品牌打入市場？

Amanda 有個很好的朋友在 Brighton 開了間可愛的小店並且要我們拿些東西在那兒寄賣。就這樣開始了。

Sanna 我們一開始在 Brighton 一個朋友的店裡賣些編織包和胸衣，那些產品被一些小雜誌注意，後來 Our Shop 的店長 Gemma [1] 跟我們聯絡，希望我們的產品能在他們店裡賣。

Liz 我們是從星期日 Up Market 開始的，基本上我們不過就是在桌上放一些自己的作品罷了！Sanna 和 Amanda 早就在一些店賣她們的產品了，對我而言卻是第一次！

1 Gemma 出現在《創意市集》第一集，她和朋友合開的店叫 Our Shop。

工作室一角

* · 妳們的產品有哪些種類？還想將觸角延伸至何處？

Amanda 我們的產品從袋子、錢包到手工編織的衣架都有，什麼種類都涉及一些。有我們自己的設計，也有一些有才華的朋友的設計。產品種類和風格有趣多樣，這也是我喜歡它的地方。

Sanna 我們有袋子、帽子、錢包、胸衣、T恤、書、徽章和卡片，還有一些我們在市集和慈善商店找到的陶器和小裝飾品。我們想將範圍擴展到家居系列，還有服裝部份，像上衣、裙子等。

Liz 我們有手工編織錢包、袋子和衣架子、布包、T恤和徽章。也有一些古典陶器。我們什麼都賣一些！

* · 請描述妳們的工作程序。

Amanda 此刻我還有全職工作，所以太陽下山後才是自我設計時光的開始！坐在沙發上邊喝茶邊工作，我家亂得要命！

Sanna 一團亂，作樣品，打樣……然後再攪和一通直到我滿意為止。

Liz 坐在電視機前吃餅乾喝茶，再做些縫紉工作！我不喜歡事前計畫太多，喜歡順其自然。

* · 妳們如何推銷並販賣妳們的產品？

Amanda 很幸運地我們在 Up Market 得到很多迴響，並且建立了許多關係。

Sanna 目前為止大多是從我們市集的攤位，我們希望能快點擁有自己的網站並且好好經營它。然後開始透過雜誌大力宣傳。

* · 從妳們開始這個品牌作業以來，讓妳們最開心的事情是什麼？最難過的呢？

Amanda 最開心的：人們美妙的迴響和反應，而且當他們來到我們攤位時通常都會微笑；希望是跟著我們一起會心一笑，而不是嘲笑我們三個人。

Sanna 不想讓妳認為我在拍馬屁，但被收錄進這本書是目前發生過最讓我開心的事！還有就是看到人們喜歡我們產品時的表情，那真的很棒！最難過的：冬天！工作室和攤位冰得像冷凍庫一樣，我很驚訝我的腳趾竟然沒有掉下來！

Liz 擁有市集攤位的好處是什麼都很立即，看到人們對我們產品的當下反應對我們而言很重要。人們經過我們的攤位，然後微笑、吃吃地笑或者針對某樣產品竊竊私語。我很喜歡這點。

* · 對於做團隊工作有什麼感想（最開心的和最痛苦的）？

Amanda 能互相丟點子的感覺很棒，而最開心的莫過於你跟別人擁有同樣的想法與熱誠。比較難過的是你得學會接受別人的想法，而且容易變得推卸責任。

Sanna 很棒，因為我們各有所長，所以我們能做任何事！有人跟你一起出主意是很棒的，即使有時它們聽來荒誕不經。

Liz 很能激發靈感，我們常一起談論想法或夢想，跟擁有相同熱忱的人在一起感覺真好。

What product range do you have? And what to expand?

Amanda   Our products range from bags, purses through to knitted coat hangers. A bit of everything. It's a great mixture of our own work and talented people we know. It's eclectic and that's what I like about it.

Sanna   Between us we have bags, hats, purses, corsages, cushions, t-shirts, books, badges and cards. As well as crockery and knick-knacks we find in markets and charity shops. Would like to increase the homeware range. And maybe a small line of clothing, e.g. tops and skirts.

Liz   We have knitted purses, bags, and coat hangers. Fabric bags, t-shirts, and badges. We also have vintage ceramics. A little of everything!

Please describe your working procedure.

Amanda   At present I am still in full time employment as well! So it's full steam ahead when the sunsets for me. It's my sofa and a lovely cuppa. My house is a mess!

Sanna   Mess about and make a prototype. Make a pattern. Mess about some more until I'm happy with it.

Liz   Sitting in front of the telly with a biscuit and a cup of tea, doing a bit of sewing! I don't really like to plan too much, I like my work to be spontaneous.

＊・ 團隊工作最重要的元素是什麼？

Amanda   溝通。

Sanna   擁有相同的幽默感。

Liz   絕對必須是擁有同樣的目標。

＊・ 妳們對 AS TWEE AS IT CAN BE 未來的期望及目標為何？

Amanda   藉由開一間店擴大營業，並且找到跟我們品味相同的人願意在我們的店裡賣他們的產品。

Sanna   征服世界！......哈哈，沒有啦！只要擁有一間附帶咖啡廳的小店就夠了。

Liz   此刻我們希望能有自己的店，工作室設在後頭，我現在都可以看見那畫面了！我們希望能找到更多擁有同樣想法的人，並且物色更多設計師。

＊・ 妳們有任何其它工作嗎？

Amanda   一間童裝工作室的織品及平面設計師。我的白天與童話做伴，晚上與編織為伍。

Sanna   現在我在一間書店做兼職工作。「現在？」，我在開誰玩笑啊！其實除了幾個自由工作案件外，我已經在書店工作了十一年！

Liz   有！我是個童裝設計師，跟 Amanda 是同事。它真是一個令人喜愛的工作，我成天都在畫狗狗、貓貓和小花！

How do you promote and sell your products?

Amanda   Luckily from Up Market we have had lots of response and made numerous contacts.

Sanna - So far mainly through the market stall. Hope to have the website up and running soon too. And then we'll start pushing for some more magazine exposure.

Since you started the brand, what has been the most joyful thing that has happened to you? And the most difficult?

Amanda   Joyful - People's amazing response. Their comments and the way everyone seems to smile at the stall... hopefully this is with us not at us.

Sanna   Without sounding like I'm sucking up... This book is probably the most exciting thing so far! And just seeing people's faces when they really love something we've made. That's pretty nice. Most difficult - Winter! The studio is like a fridge and with the stall on Sundays. I'm surprised my toes haven't dropped off!

Liz   What is good about the market stall, is that everything is so immediate. Seeing peoples reactions to what we have made is so important to us. People walk by and smile, giggle, and coo over the work. I love that.

What is it like to work as a group? (the happiest and most painful moments)

Amanda   It's great that you get to throw ideas of one another and there's nothing more encouraging than people sharing the same ideas and enthusiasm. The down side is learning to except other peoples ideas and off loading responsibility.

Sanna   It's cool because we all bring different skills to it. So between us we can do anything! And its really nice to have each other to bounce ideas off, however daft they are sometimes.

Liz   It's so inspiring, we often talk about our ideas, our dreams. It's brilliant being around people who have the same aspirations as you.

What is the most important element in working as a group?

Amanda   Communication.

Sanna   Sharing the same sense of humour!

Liz   Definitely having the same goal.

What's your vision and mission for AS TWEE AS IT CAN BE?

Amanda   To expand by opening a shop and finding more people who are as twee as ourselves and would appreciate an outlet to sell their work.

Sanna   To take over the world!...he he, not really, just to own a little shop with a cafe in it would be enough.

Liz   We eventually would like to have our own little shop, with a studio in the back. I can picture it right now! We would love to get more like minded people involved, and source new designers.

Do you have any other job?

Amanda   Textile/Graphic Designer in a childrenswear studio. It's bunnies by day and crafts by night.

Sanna   At the moment I am working part-time in a book shop. Who am I trying to kid, 'at the moment!' apart from a few big freelance jobs in between, I've worked in bookshops for the last 11 years!

Liz   Yes! I'm a childrens wear designer, I work with Amanda. It's such a lovely job, I draw dogs, and cats, and flowers all day!

* · 設計師是很難掌握的一個工作嗎？身為一位設計師感覺如何？

Amanda 即便有時腸枯思竭，我還是無法想像我能做什麼其它的工作！沒有靈感就是沒有靈感，妳無法強迫自己。那些天我總會希望自己是一名獸醫！

Sanna 我不知道 Amanda 和 Liz 如何能以它為全職工作。我發現在被要求的情況下很難讓自己有創意。

Liz 我愛死這工作了，而且我不會想做其它任何事。你一旦開始就停不下來！

* · 妳們會從以前或當代的一些設計師作品上尋找靈感嗎？

Amanda 我會從每一件人事物中找靈感。我真的覺得自己是個雜誌狂或書狂。我最迷的就是六〇和七〇年代的舊手工書籍。

Sanna 我一直都很愛 Antoni & Alison、Eley Kishimoto、Super Lovers 及 Marimekko 等牌子。

* · 妳們最喜歡的品牌或人物（可以是任何領域的）是什麼？理由為何？

Sanna 姆明家族 2！我們小時候唯一在英國家喻戶曉的芬蘭事物。我很喜歡那些書，還有它的電視影集真是又嚇人又酷！

* · 妳們還會想要挑戰哪一種行業呢？

Sanna 我對吃很有興趣，所以如果能結合食物和我們的店就太棒了，有個咖啡廳也很好。有許多許多的可口蛋糕和美味菜肴！

2 The Moomins，芬蘭藝術家兼作家 Tove Jansson 在 1940 年代所創造，有著名的姆明及哲學家姆明爸爸、手袋不離身的姆明媽媽、經常環遊世界的史力奇及頑皮的阿梅等等。

Is being a designer a difficult job to handle? How are you feeling being one?

Amanda I can't imagine ever doing anything else although I do have days where I don't have an ounce of creativity in by body! If it ain't there it just can't be forced. Those particular days I wish I was a vet!

Sanna I don't know how Amanda and Liz do it as a full-time job. I find it hard to be creative on demand.

Liz I love it, and I wouldn't want to do anything else. Once you start you can't stop!

Do you draw inspiration from the work of other artists or designers - historic or contemporary?

Amanda I draw inspiration from anything and everything. I really do believe I have a magazine and book addiction. My biggest obsession are old craft books form 60's 70's etc.

Sanna Always loved Antoni & Alison, Eley Kishimoto, Super Lovers, Marimekko.

Your favourite brand or character (can be in any category) and the reason?

Sanna The moomins! the only finnish thing that anyone in England knew when we were kids. I loved the books and the original tv series was really spooky and cool.

What other forms of business would you like to venture into one day?

Sanna I am really into food. So it would be great to combine that with our shop and have a cafe too. Lots of gorgeous cakes and savouries!

What's a typical day like for you?

Amanda Busy but fun.

Sanna Get up later than I planned, rush over to the studio for a few hours, rush back across town to the bookshop (late normally). Come home and curl up on the sofa with some sewing and the cat. (I do go out sometimes too, honest!)

Liz Well I like to start the day with a cup of tea. I catch the bus down the road to work, where I draw rabbits, fish, lions... all day. I then go home and start sewing! Very hectic, but really exciting!

What is the most inspiring thing in the world for you?

Sanna Smiley happy people.

Liz Apart from going to the Tate Modern Bookshop, I love going to car boot sales, having a good look at other peoples junk! You can find all sorts of inspiring things.

What is your favourite day of the week? And why?

Amanda Thursday, as good as Friday but without the high expectation put upon it.

Sanna Friday because even though I don't have a conventional week, everyone else is always in a happy mood, and it makes for a good day!

Liz Monday, a start to a new week.

What is your least favourite day of the week? And why?

Amanda Wednesday, neither the beginning or the end.

Sanna Wednesday, because it always comes around too quick and you realise the week's half gone already!

Liz Wednesday, it's so in between!

What do you do to kill time?

Amanda I have no time.

Sanna Never need to, it always disappears anyway!

Liz Day dream!

※‧ 平常妳們都是如何度過一天的？

Amanda 忙碌但有趣。

Sanna 比預定中晚起、匆匆趕到工作室做幾個小時、匆匆跨越到位在倫敦另一頭的書店工作（通常會遲到）、再回家蜷縮在沙發上做些縫紉工作和陪貓玩（我有時也會出門，真的！）

Liz 我喜歡喝杯茶來開始我的一天，我在路的那一頭搭公車去上班，在那裡我整天畫兔子、魚、獅子等。然後回家，開始縫紉！非常累，卻也非常有趣。

※‧ 對妳們來說，全世界最能激發妳們靈感的東西是什麼？

Amanda 愛笑的快樂人們！

Liz 除了到泰德當代藝術館 (Tate Modern) 的書店之外，我喜歡逛逛車庫拍賣，仔細地看看別人不要的東西是什麼！你會在那裡看到一堆最能激發你靈感的東西。

※‧ 一星期中妳們最喜歡哪一天？為什麼？

Amanda 星期四，跟喜歡星期五一樣多，但不會期望那麼高。

Sanna 星期五，即便我不像一般人過規律的一週，我四周的人在這天都開開心心的，這就可以造就美好的一天！

Liz 星期一，一星期的開始。

※‧ 一星期中妳們最討厭的一天呢？為什麼？

Amanda 星期三，既不是開始又不是結束。

Sanna 星期三，因為它總是來得那麼快，讓我發現一個星期已經過了一半了！

Liz 星期三，太中間地帶了。

※‧ 妳們都怎麼打發時間？

Amanda 我沒時間。

Sanna 從不需要，反正它總是消失不見！

Liz 做白日夢！

sneaked o... early smiling to herself the

They were both thinking the same thing. but Sometimes it's not really worth it

※ · 妳們最喜愛和最討厭倫敦哪一點？

Amanda　我喜歡它的多樣性，任何事都有自己的文化存在。我討厭時而無禮的人們（天啊我快變成老小姐了）。

Sanna　喜歡：它的氣氛，各種不同的人事物，還有那些可愛、頗富特色的地區（Hampstead、Stoke Newington 等地）。討厭：臭味和滿地的垃圾、髒鼻涕，以及交通擁擠到去哪都困難的時刻。

Liz　我喜歡坐公車，你可以在公車上看到各種人事物！這也是我討厭地鐵的原因，它又暗又臭！

※ · 妳們的聖典？

Amanda　我的室友 Valerie 的黃金萬能雙手！

Sanna　我好像沒有......這樣會不會讓我聽來像個無神論者？

Liz　Charlotte Solomon 的 *Life? or Theatre?*。她是個畫家，每天用畫來寫日記。她會把今天發生過的事和人們説的話寫下來，真的很美，很深入內心。我想這影響了我的設計和想法很多。

※ · 妳們最近在讀些什麼書？內容為何？

Amanda　*Craft and Art: The Business*。

Sanna　William M. Thackeray 的 *Vanity Fair*。一個女孩如何在社會上爬升自己的地位。

Liz　*Style City New York*。讀這本是因為我很快就要去一趟了，耶！

※ · 當工作或思考遇到瓶頸時，妳們都怎麼做？

Amanda　先走開，並且希望回來再看一次時能有全新觀點。

Sanna　休息一下吃吃點心。

Liz　跟任何願意聽我説話的人聊聊！然後一試再試直到行得通為止。

※ · 妳們如何應付壓力？

Amanda　編織......我是個挺水平式的人（附註：喜歡躺在床上那種）。

Sanna　吃零嘴！

Liz　我喜歡去一間叫 Twenty Twenty One 的小店逛，它總是能讓我感覺好過些，不然就是喝杯茶吃塊蛋糕。

工作室一角

※ · 妳們現在過的是夢想中的生活嗎？如果不是，妳們夢想中的生活型態及地點為何？

Amanda 我是過著我夢想中的生活！但如果有家人在身邊會覺得更完美。

Sanna 我喜歡西班牙式生活，很愜意。但同時我又很想住在很有活力的紐約！

Liz 我喜歡目前的生活，但我想很快地我必須只做兼職工作，這樣才能花更多時間在 AS TWEE AS IT CAN BE 上。如果我們都能把全部的時間精力花在它上面將會是很棒的一件事。開間店，而工作室就在後頭，棒極了！

※ · 讓妳們維持生活步調及常規的事物是什麼？

Amanda 家人朋友。

Sanna 不斷開著的收音機和足夠的零嘴。

Liz Elle Decoration 雜誌，那是我的最愛！

※ · 妳們最喜歡的飲料、音樂類型及電影各是什麼？

Amanda 飲料：茶；音樂：視我心情而定，從桃莉芭頓到 Le Tigre 都好；電影：《天涯赤子心》(The Champ)……好感人喔！

Sanna Gin Tonic；北方靈魂樂及《飛越杜鵑窩》(One Flew Over the Cuckoo's Nest)。

Liz 此刻最喜歡薄荷茶；電影則是 Buffalo 66。

What's your bible?
Amanda Valerie my housemates Golden Hands!
Sanna I don't think I have one... does that make me an atheist?
Liz Charlotte Solomon's 'Life? or Theatre?'. She is an artist who made a visual diary of every day of her life. Everyday she would paint what happened to her, what people had said... It's so beautiful, and very personal. I think this has very much influenced my work and my ideas.

What book are you reading at the moment? And what's it about?
Amanda Craft and Art - The Business.
Sanna Vanity Fair by Thackeray, a young girl who manipulates her way up society.
Liz Style City New York. I'm reading this because I'm going very soon for a while, Yippee!

What do you love and hate the most about London?
Amanda I love the diversity, cultures the way you have access to everything. I hate peoples lack of manners sometimes (God I'm turning into an old lady).
Sanna Love - the atmosphere, variety of people and things to do, the little villagey areas (Hampstead, Stoke Newington, etc). Hate - smell and litter, black snot and the hour that it takes to get anyway!
Liz I love sitting on Buses, you can see all sorts of things from a bus! That's why I hate the tube, it's dark, and smelly!

What do you do when you are stuck on a particular design/idea?
Amanda Walk away and hope when I return I have a different outlook on it.
Sanna Take a snack break.
Liz I talk to anyone who will listen! And I keep trying until it works!

How do you handle your stress?
Amanda Knit... I'm pretty horizontal though (my note: lie in bed).
Sanna Snack!
Liz I like to go to a lovely shop like Twenty Twenty One, it always makes me feel better, or I just have a cup of tea and a cake.

Are you living your ideal lifestyle right now? If not, what's your ideal lifestyle & place to be?
Amanda I am living it! Although if my family were here to that would be perfect.
Sanna I love the spanish way of life. So laidback but on the flip-side I'd also love to live in new york, for the energy!
Liz I like how things are going, but I think soon I need to work part time, so I can devote more time to AS TWEE AS CAN BE. It would be really good to get to the point where we can work on AS TWEE AS CAN BE all the time. Open the shop, and have a studio in the back, lovely!

What keeps you going and stay in tune?
Amanda Family, friends.
Sanna Radio in the background and an ample supply of snack food.
Liz Elle Decoration, it's my favourite thing!

What's your favourite drink, music & film?
Amanda Drink - Tea. Music - Depends on my mood anything from Dolly Parton to Le Tigre. Film - The Champ.....oh how I cry.
Sanna Gin & tonic, northern soul music & one flew over the cuckoo's nest.
Liz At the moment it's Mint Tea, and the film 'Buffalo 66'.

＊・ 怎麼樣會特別討妳們開心？
Sanna 讓我放鬆或停止思考一下下，或者乾脆讓我隨著美妙音樂起舞直到腳皮磨破為止！
Liz 到我奶奶位在森林裡的家，然後吃片好吃的自製胡蘿蔔蛋糕。

＊・ 妳們平時都怎麼烹調馬鈴薯？
Amanda 我不烹調，我通常就是買一包現成的，在上頭放些調味料、脆片什麼的。
Sanna 我好愛馬鈴薯！烤馬鈴薯、馬鈴薯泥、烘馬鈴薯、馬鈴薯片、炒馬鈴薯！任何妳想得到的方法！上帝最棒的發明！
Liz 我喜歡把它們水煮一下，然後撒點鹽巴放在烤箱裡烘，嗯～～

＊・ 夢想中的工作是？
Amanda 我現在正在做的工作......不過要避免過於自大的態度。
Sanna 任何錢賺最多、事情最少的工作，不過很遺憾地我選了完全相反的一個。
Liz 擁有我們自己的店面！

＊・ 什麼是妳們從沒嘗試過、但哪一天一定會去做的事？
Amanda 唱卡拉ＯＫ。
Sanna 騎部摩托車，也許只是小小的一台，甚至小綿羊 (Moped) 也好。
Liz 攀岩！

＊・ 妳們最近迷些什麼東西？
Amanda 玻璃廣口瓶和陶器。
Sanna 冰淇淋蘇打。
Liz 紐約......我等不及要去了！

What would be a special treat for you?

Sanna To be able to relax and stop thinking for a short while or alternatively to dance my socks off to some really good music!

Liz Going to my Nan's house in the forest, and having a slice of home made carrot cake!

What's your usual way of cooking potato?

Amanda I don't. I usually buy them in a bag with some a bit of flavouring... crisps.

Sanna I love potatoes!!! Roasted, mashed, baked, chipped, sauteed! Everyway you can! God's most versatile creation.

Liz I like to boil them for a bit, then bake them in the oven with a little bit of salt...mmm.

A dream job to you is...

Amanda Exactly what I am doing now... without sounding too smug.

Sanna One that provides the most money for the least effort! but unfortunately I've chosen the opposite!

Liz Having our very own shop!

What have you not tried to do, but would definitely want to try one day?

Amanda Karoke.

Sanna Ride a motorbike, but probably just a little one, or even a moped.

Liz Rock Climbing!

What is your latest obsession?

Amanda Glass jars and crockery.

Sanna Ice cream sodas.

Liz New York... I can't wait to go!!

What can't you live without?

Amanda Family friends... chessy I know but oh so true.

Sanna Snacks and cats.

Liz Chocolate.

Please describe yourself in a short sentence.

Amanda Quietly confident, too organised and a big softie.

Sanna Scatty, petite brunette into music, films and picnics would like to meet cute boy for kicks and giggles!

Liz Scatty! Silly and a little loopy

Dare to share one of your secrets?

Amanda I love Spam.

Sanna They're all far too dark!

Liz Newark Antiques Market every few months, a fantastic source of inspiration!

Dream to be...

Amanda Out of student debt.

Sanna Contented.

＊· 妳們生活中不可或缺的東西為何？

Amanda 家人朋友，很老套的答案我知道，但卻是真的。

Sanna 零嘴和貓。

Liz 巧克力。

＊· 請用簡單的一句話形容妳們自己。

Amanda 沉默的自信，太條理分明，極端敏感。

Sanna 喜愛音樂、電影和野餐的、瘋狂又嬌小的棕髮女郎，想要尋找志同道合的可愛男孩！

Liz 糊塗、瘋狂和一點點神經病！

＊· 要不要跟大家分享妳們的祕密？

Amanda 我喜歡吃罐頭豬肉。

Sanna 它們太見不得人了！

Liz 每隔幾個月舉辦一次的紐渥克古董市場 (Newark Antiques Market) 是很棒的靈感來源。

＊· 夢想能......

Amanda 早日擺脫學生貸款。

Sanna 知足常樂。

Eleanor Patricia Logan

Eleanor Patricia Logan (Elliemay)

elliemaylogan@hotmail.com
sell at Sunday (Up) Market.
studio address_95 Hanley road, Finsbury park , n4 3DQ London

Elliemay 畫的女孩兒們

Elliemay 是個能帶給你很多想像空間的女人......那天我在 Up Market 後面的角落看見她，身材高挑，綁著兩條長長的辮子，身上披著一件超厚的白色毛皮外套，及膝長裙、長靴，戴著一頂東北人的毛帽，有點異類，可是頗具特色的打扮。起初我以為她賣的是手稿繪圖，走近仔細一看才發現它們是攝影作品。和平常攝影作品不同的是，照片中的場景與內容皆由她的手繪圖畫剪紙構成：她將畫好的人物剪下來，穿插安排在不同的故事場景之中，然後打燈拍照。這讓我興奮地想起小時候玩紙娃娃扮家家酒，自己幻想、編故事，那些充滿一人對白、扮演多種角色的遊戲。

Elliemay 畫中的主角絕大多數都是性感、線條優美的女人；照片中的光線讓景深前後分明，充滿戲劇張力。她說自己的作品一直都有戲劇性的成分存在，這可能是因為小時候經常跟著父母出入劇院看表演，所以不知不覺在創作中，也會將自己的情緒和感覺融合，藉由這種方式表現出來。

來自紐西蘭，Elliemay 的人跟她的作品一樣，充滿戲劇性。她說話的語調不急不緩，有種安定力，有時你會覺得她好像訴說的是別人的故事。從小我行

我素，想做什麼就做什麼的個性，一直是個讓父母耽心的小孩。特立獨行的她走過很多地方，從印度到南韓；做過各式各樣的工作，從櫃台小姐到英文老師。她說她喜歡做連自己都摸不著頭緒的事情，內心經常衍生出不同的渴望，而這些渴望促使她不斷地變動。但從小唯一沒變過的是藝術對她的吸引力：從有記憶開始，她就愛畫畫，對她來說，拿起筆畫圖就像呼吸一般自然。

2004年3月 Elliemay 來到倫敦，好自由的一個地方！開放的風氣讓她得到一種前所未有的歸屬感，即使用再另類的方式去表達藝術作品也不會有人抱以異樣的眼光。為了生活，她開始在市集中賣紐西蘭傳統服裝和她的攝影作品，結果沒想到她的作品的銷售成績遠遠超出紐西蘭傳統服裝。欣賞與肯定的評價接踵而來，給了她對創作藝術的信心和向前的推動力。撰寫這本書的同時，Elliemay 正在紐西蘭幫一個英國服裝品牌開拓市場（又是一個不同的工作！），但是記得和她聊天時她很認真的說著，希望有一天能全心全意投入她的繪畫和藝術；因為只有在做這件事的時候，她的心才是 100% 安定，不再渴望變動的時刻。

﹡·跟我們聊聊妳的作品及藝術,妳是如何想出整個概念的?

我大約在五年前開始迷上攝影……而且我一直都在畫女孩,以女孩為主軸的各種呈現方式來創造一個奇幻世界。

﹡·透過妳的作品妳表達了些什麼?

我透過線條表現當下的情緒,如果我感到憤怒,那麼我畫出來的線條會較尖銳,女孩們的肢體語言就會顯得呆板僵硬;放鬆的情緒則用開放及垂落的肩膀來表達。

﹡·請介紹一下妳自己並說明妳的背景。

我從懂得握筆時就在畫畫了,而且一直喜歡畫女孩。十四歲那年我為一間法國學校的作業案件畫了生平第一部動畫,其實無論做什麼事我總是盡情去發揮創造力。之後我在時裝店工作,受到流行服飾業及一些插畫家的啟發,像是 Erte[1],然後上學、到世界各地旅行。印度當地的小型油畫及不同國家運用色彩的方式給了我不少靈感。我是紐西蘭人,那裡的光線又亮又白,所以我比較喜歡亞洲國家的金色光線。

在到印度、泰國和歐洲各地旅行之間,我也同時完成了世界宗教的學位。我做了很多奇奇怪怪的工作,從逐戶拜訪的推銷員到在蘇格蘭經營一家 B&B 旅館[2]。

然後我在紐西蘭投入了音樂工業,參與造型設計及音樂海報繪製,也因而奠定了我的剪紙風格。時尚和音樂工業令我著迷,所以在我二十多歲時

都在這個領域工作,之後我去了南韓邊緣的一個小島,在那住了十五個月。

去年我搬到倫敦,開始了我的市集生涯,並且在倫敦 Bricklane 的一間美國復古舊物店工作,然後又在 Carnaby 街上的一間設計師精品店兼差,開始做更多發揮創意的事情,像是商品陳列及櫥窗展示。

今年初我還為這家服裝店到柏林參加 Bread & Butter 商展,去展示我們新一季的服裝系列,成績很好;因此他們也希望我能到澳洲去幫他們銷售二個月。現在,我必須在繪畫及時裝業之間做個選擇,因為我的藝術作品在市集中賣得很好,有本雜誌也即將刊登我的作品……我很想去跟隨著興趣走……但不得不為了生活面對現實……希望有一天能為自己作畫,而不是只為了賺錢。時尚界很有趣,但並非我心所屬,從它身上賺錢倒是比較容易;但藝術是我投注了非常多情感的東西,所以下任何有關它的決定總是要花比較多的時間。

1 原名 Roman de Tirtoff,出生於俄國,他以法語發音的名字縮寫 Erte 享譽藝術界,同時也是20世紀初著名的時裝和舞台設計大師。
2 Bed & Breakfast,提供床舖和早餐的家庭旅館。

Tell us about your works & art. How did you come up with the concept?
About 5 years ago, I got interested in photography... and as I had always drawn girls, and girls played with different mediums to create more of a fantastical universe.

What are you expressing through your works?
I express my emotion at the time with line, if I am feeling angry, the lines will be sharp and the body language of the girl will express stiffness, or openness and dropped shoulders say for a relaxed emotion.

Please introduce yourself & tell us about your background.
I have drawn since I was able to pick up a pen and always drew girls. At 14 I made my first animation for a French school project, somehow I was always getting in my want for being creative no matter what subject I had to take. Later I worked in fashion shops and became inspired by the fashion/clothing medium and illustrators who have also been, like Erte. I lived and went to school then travelled to many places in the world. India miniature painting has been an inspiration as have the colours used in other countries.
I am from New Zealand where the light is very bright and white so I love the more golden lights of some Asian countries.

So amongst travel to India, Thailand, UK, Europe, I got a degree in world religions and then did many strange and varied jobs from door-to-door sales to running a bed and breakfast in Scotland.

I then worked on music production in New Zealand, helping with the styling and drawing for music posters and cultivating my current cut out style.

The fashion/music world fascinated me, so I ended up doing work in this area in my 20's and then living for 15 months on an island off the bottom of South Korea.

Just last year I moved to London, where I started a market stall, worked in an American vintage warehouse off Bricklane in London, then at a designer's boutique just off Carnaby Street.

I have found myself doing more creative work here doing visual merchandising and window displays.

Earlier this year I went to the Berlin BREAD & BUTTER trade show to sell our fashion collection.

We did very well, and I got a job now to sell to Australasia for 2 months. I had to choose between my illustration and fashion world for now, as the art was selling very well at the market and I have work coming out in a magazine... so I would like to go with the omentum, but I need to make a living!... then I can draw for myself... rather than do it just for the money. The fashion world I have fun in, but it's not as personal for me, so it's easier to make money from., whereas my art is something I get very emotional about... so it takes longer to make decisions about what to do with it.

How did you first become aware of and become interested in art?

My parents took me to A LOT of theatre and opera. An early memory of a french company, I think... they did visual illusion on stage with a lot of black and white graphics by simple movements of boards on stage has stayed with me. Paddington Bear in England I liked too... the cut out nature and simplicity of it was inspiring. I like Black and white and cut outs because I like reading a book, as opposed to watching a movie, it allows you to fill in your own feelings and thoughts... it's more open to interpretation. My father and I would look through big colour art books on Sunday afternoons after mum's amazing Sunday lunch. He would fiddle with my ear and I would enjoy my parents being relaxed and would while away the afternoon looking and feeling and imagining the story of the pictures. These books were old masters through to modernism. In my late teens I liked the German expressionists - the strong reds and greens... Funnily now I like black and white! I also like Giotto and old Italian religious paintings because of the gold and blue... I then became more and more personal with etchings and stage like falt 2d/3d pictures like the old religious pictures and also Chinese dinner plates with the blue and white simple colour but very detailed story like maze of description of a picture say of a bride and house and some ladies in robes. As a kid I spent time looking at my parents vast art collection... I spent a lot of time alone doing this.

* · 妳是怎麼注意到藝術並且開始對它產生興趣的？

我父母帶我看了很多很多的戲劇和歌劇，有個很早以前的印象，我想是法國某劇團……那些人在台上運用各種簡單的動作來移動許多繪有黑、白圖像的板塊，藉此造成人們的視覺錯置，這個印象一直停留在我腦海裡。

我也很喜歡英國的派丁頓熊 (Paddington Bear)，它的圖像拼貼自然簡潔，給我不少啟發。我喜歡黑色、白色和拼貼風格，因為就像看書或看電影，它讓你填滿個人的感覺和思想，讓你能隨自己的想法去解釋。

小時候我跟爸爸會在媽咪可口的星期天午餐後閱讀大本、色彩豐富的藝術相關書籍，爸爸會玩玩我的耳朵，一起消磨時光，我很喜歡父母這麼放鬆的感覺，整個下午我們都在細看、體會、並且想像圖畫書中的故事。那些書全是現代主義的先驅。

青少年後期我喜歡上德國的表現主義——充斥著強烈的紅色和綠色，好玩的是我現在喜歡黑和白。我也很喜歡喬托 (Giotto di bondone, 1267-1337) 和古義大利時期的宗教油畫——因為它們飽合的金色和藍色。之後我愈來愈喜歡蝕刻畫和古代宗教油畫，及中國磁盤上的 2D 及 3D 圖，它們用藍色及其它簡單的色彩，卻能不可思議地描述出一個關於新嫁娘、她的家庭及穿著長袍的古代仕女的詳盡故事。

我的童年在觀賞我爸媽大量的藝術收藏中渡過，獨處的大部份時間都在做這些。

在 Up Market 的攤位

Elliemay 家中自設的小攝影桌

＊‧妳畫的角色中有妳自己存在嗎？
我總是存在於我的角色中，大家都這麼想，所以
應該有吧！

＊‧妳如何描述自己的藝術風格？
在攝影中加入玩弄剪影、光線和空間的 2D 及 3D
風格。

＊‧請描述一下妳的工作程序。
八小時繪畫，四小時剪貼，設定好場景，拍攝，
沖印。

＊‧妳如何推銷並販賣妳的產品？
倫敦 Bricklane 的市集；隨時展示給人們看；透
過 www.pimpguides.com 網站。

＊‧妳對妳工作的未來期望及目標為何？
嘗試去完成我所有的夢想。

＊‧從妳開始這個工作以來，讓妳最開心的事情是什麼？
最難過的呢？
最開心的——當我的作品印製出來的那個「藝術
時刻」，我會用不同的角度去看，並且發現它跟
原先不同而且比我想像中還要來得好時。

最難過的——我曾經召集了一批藝術家來繪製一
個以當地樂團為主題的聖誕卡系列，結果不小心
印太多，於是在所有的辛苦和努力過後我不但什
麼都沒拿到，還得自掏腰包付錢給所有參與的藝
術家，而且還讓人覺得我沒有盡力，不在乎……
為此我難過了好幾年。

＊‧妳有任何其它工作嗎？
一個倫敦時裝品牌的澳洲市場負責人。

Is there a part of you in the characters you draw?
Always a part of me in my characters... people always think so... so it must be so.

How would you describe your style of art?
2D/3D cut out illustration playing with shadow, light and space in the medium of photography.

Please describe your working procedure.
8 hours drawing, 4 hours cutting out, setting up a set, photograph, printing.

How do you promote and sell your works?
Market, Bricklane London; show people when I can; www.pimpguides.com.

What's your vision and mission for the future of your works?
To attempt ALL my dreams.

What has been the most joyful thing that has happened to you since you started this work? And the most difficult?
Most joyful - Art moment whenever I see my work in print, I get to see it with different angles... It somehow looks different and better than I thought it did.

Most difficult - I started up a Christmas card series organising artists to depict a local band. Too many cards got printed by mistake, so I made no profit and had to pay the artists out of my own pocket after a lot of hard work, and felt it looked as if I didn't care... I felt bad about it for years.

Do you have any other job?
A london fashion label rep for Australia.

What was the strangest job you ever had?
Dressing in traditional Thai clothes as a New Zealand girl working in a restaurant in Scotland.

Is being an artist difficult job to handle? How are you feeling being one?
Being an artist is difficult... but it is like love... if you preserve, it's the most rewarding thing in your life.

Your favourite brand or character (can be in any category) and the reason?
Noodoll world!

What would you be doing if you weren't doing what you are doing now?
I would possibly be a teacher.

What other forms of business would you like to venture into one day?
Stage design.

What's a typical day like for you?
Work at a fashion shop 5 days, a shoe shop 1 day and the market selling my art on the 7th. When I have a day off I make new art. Part of the year I travel to sell the fashion label to Australia.

What is the most inspiring thing in the world for you?
Sandy Jeffs who made and runs a shop called Frutti in Wellington, New Zealand because she is open to new ideas, she travels often to buy materials for her shop, she designs, she assists others with their dreams... and is always colourful, she always wears happy positive clothes. She has a man, two daughters and a house that overlooks the sea, and her own studio high on the hill. She is non-pretentious and gets energy from being inspired by her environment. I want to be like that.

＊ 妳做過最奇怪的工作是什麼？
身為一個紐西蘭女孩，卻必須在蘇格蘭一家餐廳裡穿著泰國傳統服裝工作。

＊ 藝術家是很難掌握的一個工作嗎？身為一位藝術家的感覺如何？
身為一名藝術家的確很難，但這就跟愛一樣，只要好好珍惜，它就是你生命中最值得的東西。

＊ 妳最喜歡的牌子或人物（可以是任何領域的）以及理由？
Noodoll World！

＊ 如果不是做這行妳會從事什麼工作？
舞台設計。

＊ 跟大家描述妳的一天。
五天在時裝店工作，一天在鞋店工作，剩下的一天在市集賣我的作品。休假的時候我會做些新的作品，一年當中會花些時間到澳洲行銷我服務的時裝品牌。

＊ 對妳來說，全世界最能激發妳靈感的東西是什麼？
Sandy Jeffs 在紐西蘭威靈頓經營的店 Frutti。她是個能接受新的想法的人，經常到世界各地去旅行，採買店裡需要的材料。她設計，也幫助別人完成夢想，而且總是色彩繽紛的夢想……她的穿著花俏自信。她有丈夫、兩個女兒和一間可以俯視海灘的房子，工作室則設在山坡上。她自然不造作，從獲得靈感的四周環境中得到動力。我也希望像她這樣。

Elliemay 的攝影作品

* · 一星期中妳最喜愛哪一天？理由為何？
  星期六，我也不知道為什麼。

* · 一星期中妳最討厭哪一天？理由為何？
  星期六，我也不知道為什麼。

* · 妳都怎麼打發時間？
  從來沒有時間可以打發。

* · 妳奉行不渝的守則是什麼？
  我的守則是緣份。來去隨緣的原則。

* · 妳此刻讀些什麼書？書的內容是什麼？
  我書讀得不好，所以都不讀，不過我想改變這個
  習慣。

* · 妳最喜愛和最討厭倫敦哪一點？
  喜愛的一點──它從不令人覺得無聊，我總是很
  興奮地起床期待每天將會發生的新鮮事物！
  討厭的一點──人們在人行道上吐痰。

* · 當工作或思考遇到瓶頸時妳都怎麼做？
  當我遇到瓶頸時我會先做另一件工作，之後再回
  頭來做這件事，或者乾脆完全不管它，順其自然
  最好。

* · 妳如何應付妳的壓力？
  生氣，哭泣，然後覺得很累，然後我的男友
  Reuben 會聽我抱怨，逗我取笑自己。然後我會
  重新振作，想些別的方法來進行工作。

* · 妳現在過的是妳夢想中的生活嗎？如果不是，妳夢想
  中的生活型態和地點為何？
  在三個國家都有房子、賺足夠的錢好讓我有時間
  繪畫和展覽。擁有一間工作室，並且幫助別人瞭
  解他們的夢想。

* · 妳最喜歡的飲料、音樂類型和電影是什麼？
  最喜歡喝紅酒，最喜歡的電影是《1984》，最喜
  歡的音樂類型──很糟的流行音樂、靈魂樂、爵
  士樂及迪斯可！

What is your favourite day of the week? And why?
Saturday. I don't know why.

What is your least favourite day of the week? And why?
Saturday. I don't know why.

What do you do to kill time?
Never have any to kill.

What's your bible?
My bible, is karma. What comes around goes around principle.

What book are you reading at the moment? And what's it about?
I ain't read very well, so don't, but would like to change that.

What do you love and hate the most about London?
Love about London - It's NEVER boring, always excited to wake up to see whats in store!! Hate - people spitting in the pavement.

What do you do when you are stuck on a particular piece of work/idea?
When I'm stuck on a piece, I start something new and come back to it or completely leave it, as I like flow.

How do you handle your stress?
Get angry then cry then feel tired then my partner Reuben listens and makes me laugh at myself, then I collect myself, make a plan to do things a bit differently then carry on.

Are you living your ideal lifestyle right now? If not, what's your ideal lifestyle & place to be?
Having 3 countries as home and making enough money to have time to draw and exhibit, have a studio, and to be able to help others realise their dreams.

What's your favourite drink, music & film?
Favourite drink red wine. Film - 1984. Music - terrible pop music and soul/jazz/DISCO!!!

What would be a special treat for you?
To drink beer and eat german sausages in the sun by the lake in germany.

What's your usual way of cooking potatoes?
Baked potato.

A dream job to you is...
Travel, meeting people, creating art works in different countries.

What have you not tried to do, but would definitely want to try one day?
Fashion design.

What is your latest obsession?
Keeping my receipts! and filing them.

What can't you live without?
Lots of water a day.

Please describe yourself in a short sentence.
Energetic, positive, eager, risk-taking, will preserve, make mistakes but always get back up again.

Dare to share one of your secrets?
I'm open, and happy to tell people my weak points, so that they feel comfortable to be themselves around me.

Dream to be...
An artist full time.

※ · 怎麼樣會特別討妳開心？
在德國的湖邊，陽光下，請我喝啤酒吃德國香腸。

※ · 妳通常都怎麼烹調馬鈴薯？
烘培。

※ · 夢想中的工作是？
旅行、交朋友，在不同的國家從事藝術工作。

※ · 什麼是妳從沒有嘗試過、但有一天一定會去做的一件事？
服裝設計。

※ · 最近迷些什麼東西？
收集所有的收據，然後分類！

※ · 什麼是妳生活中不可或缺的？
每天喝很多水。

※ · 請用簡單的一句話來形容妳自己。
有活力、正向思考、熱心、愛冒險、珍惜事物、知錯能改。

※ · 要不要跟大家分享妳的祕密？
我很開朗，並且樂意跟人們談論我的缺點，所以人們在我身邊總是可以自在的做自己。

※ · 夢想能……
做個全職藝術家。

GLOBALUNIVERSALINTERRACIALWORLDWIDEPAN
INTERCONTINENTALTRANSATLANTICOMNIPRES
BROWNBABY.

WORLDWIDEPAN-PACIF
OMNIPRESENTA

MISC.

Toby Laurent

www.misc.me.uk
toby@misc.me.uk
sell at London Portobello Market (Saturday) & Spitalfield's
Market (Sunday)

THIS IS HARDCORE

密室中的客廳

Toby 的貓王 T 恤作品

倫敦，有各色各樣的人種，白人黑人黃種人巧克力人麥片人，再加上混到都已經不知道 CMYK 怎麼調的混血兒；光是「看人」這個活動就可以自成一個倫敦旅遊行程。我想，混血兒特別美的原因來自於他們基因中參雜著的不同顏色、性格，再混合他們成長過成中所接收的不同文化和背景，讓他們在外人眼中多了一層神秘感。這篇文章的主角就是 'BrownBaby'（棕色寶寶），Toby 這樣稱呼他自己。

黑白混血，Toby 長得很好看，健康的膚色和身材，一頭編著辮子的長髮，看起來比較像玩音樂的人。訪問他之前我在不同的市集看過他幾次，他賣的是自己設計的 T恤。每次看見 Toby 雖然總是匆匆一瞥，但對他印象深刻，因為他有時候看起來活力充沛，有時候卻異常的安靜，這兩種情緒他很不一樣，讓我不禁好奇他的作品到底是不是也像他一樣混合著這麼不同的情緒。

他製作的 T恤，不是歸類在把漂亮的圖案印上去就OK 的那種 T恤，而是每一件都抒發出不同的訊息：有對政治的嘲諷，有對社會、文化、人物、種族和音樂

的想法表達。Toby 是一個有自己想法的人，三年前厭倦了朝久晚五規律的上班生活，在朋友的鼓勵下自創 T恤品牌 MISC.。很自然地選擇市集做他創意事業的起點，純粹是因為他生長於 Portobello Market 附近，對整個市集環境很熟悉。媽媽也是藝術家，所以承襲了藝術天份也不是 surprise。我們偶爾會相約一起去看展覽，所以除了他的作品之外我對他又多了一層了解。

Toby 的人生觀是努力工作，努力玩；他喜歡認識朋友，喜歡表達自己，我覺得他是那種從表達自己之中去探索自己，進而更加了解自己的人。身為混血兒的他，在成長過程中也困惑於身處兩種文化與種族之間的衝突，曾經把頭髮整頭染金，曾經難以定位自己。在他很多的作品中經常提到種族根基的重要性，這些感觸都是來自於他曾經的困惑。他也花很多時間思考，從以往的疑惑到現在以混血兒的身分自豪；對每件事，他都會不斷思索追尋直到真正了解為止，而畫畫、設計則提供了一個渲洩想法的出口。「我想我永遠都會從事和藝術創作有關的事，不論是以那種管道來表達。」Toby 自信、篤定的說著……

賣得最好的一件作品

Toby 的 T恤圖案作品

＊· 跟我們聊聊 MISC. 這個牌子吧！你如何想出這個產
品名稱及概念？

在我的電腦桌面上，我的設計往往都會被存放入
"misc." 這個檔案匣中。對我而言，misc.[1] 這個
名字在我用創作靈感填滿它之前，都是空洞無意
義的。好的東西總是躲在這個隨處可見的字眼後
頭，而且這個字很隨性，字義也會隨著我的作品
而改變。

＊· 你透過 MISC. 想要表達些什麼？

某種程度上我想抓住某些跟我們息息相關的事
物，有些比起其它的要來得更加私人、或更特定
的事物。環境、政治、社會、音樂、設計，所有
構成「文化」的事物。

＊· 你設計的 T恤中你最喜歡的系列為何？

全都喜歡。

1 misc. 是 miscellaneous 的簡寫，多樣化的意思。

＊· 你是如何將這個品牌打入市場的？

我在倫敦西區的 Portobello Market 設了個攤位，
就開始賣了。

＊· 請介紹你自己並且跟大家說說你的背景。

哈囉，我是 Toby Laurent Belson，在倫敦西區出
生長大──曾有一年的時間因為太嚮往大自然而
住在國外。從小就憑藉紙筆去盡情表達思維，被
灌輸對抗柴契爾政府的意識、被教導如何像馬丁
路德一樣去戰鬥的勇氣和精神，是一個心存感激
的黑白混血兒。

＊· 你是何時第一次意識到自己對設計有興趣？

我在充滿油畫和素描的藝術環境下，由母親及外
婆扶養長大，畫畫是我記憶所及第一件讓我感到
自傲的事。

Tell us a bit about MISC. How did you come up
with the name and concept?
My designs always end up in the 'misc.' folder on my
computer desktop. For me, that name is empty, until I
support it with something that excites me. The good
stuff is all behind a word that exists everywhere you
look. It's very random, I suppose, and the meaning of
the name changes, as I produce more work behind it.

What are you expressing through MISC.?
I try to tackle issues that concern us all, to some
degree. Some are more personal, or specific, than
others. The environment. Politics. Society. Music.
Design. All the things that define a culture.

What's your favourite themes for the t-shirts?
Everything.

How did you launch the brand onto the market?
I got myself a stall on Portobello Market, in West
London, and started selling.

Please introduce yourself & tell us about your
background.
Hello, my name is Toby Laurent Belson. Born and
raised in West London-with a year out in the country
for extra sensitivity to nature. Given paper and pencil
to express myself in the best way. Given Margaret
Thatcher as an example of what to fight. Given Martin
Luther King Jnr as an example of how to fight.
A BrownBaby thanks to people mixing.

How did you first become aware of and become
interested in design?
My Mother and Grandmother brought me up surrounded
by paintings and drawings. Drawing was the first
thing I had regular feelings of pride about.

Toby 的家

* · 你如何形容你的設計風格？
  不知道耶，你説呢？

* · 你會擴大你產品的觸角及種類嗎？
  在我可以負擔的範圍之內。製造新的東西總是樂
  趣無窮，觸及更多產品種類意味著我有學習新的
  方法和練習的機會，這對任何行業來説都是重要
  的一個步驟。

* · 你對 MISC. 的期望及目標為何？
  成為一個促進及描繪出更好的生活的推手，提醒
  人們對他人的責任。用全方位的設計來讓產品更
  好，而不是只有「更快」、「更高」、「更大」
  或「更小」。

* · 你賣得最好的設計是哪一項？理由呢？
  「相信我，古柯鹼真的很棒，它造就了今天的
  我」，模仿美國總統喬治・布希口氣的杜撰名
  言。我想這個設計受歡迎是因為它引用了全世界
  最備受爭議、集結了恨意與荒謬的經典人物，牽
  涉毒品，而且設計簡單、強烈。

* · 你最喜歡的設計是哪一項？為什麼？
  全部都愛，它們都是我的孩子。哈哈！

* · 從你開始這個品牌作業以來，讓你感到最開心的事情
  是什麼？最難過的呢？
  最開心的是與人交流；最難過的是尚未發揮它的
  潛力。

* · 你穿不穿自己設計的衣服？
  一直都穿，這是擔任設計師最大的好處之一。

* · 設計師是很難掌握的一個工作？身為一位設計師感覺
  如何？
  有時很難，因為你不斷在展示自己的作品、成
  果，並且藉此來審視自己。説實在的，我並沒有
  將自己定位為一名設計師。我透過設計來表現自
  己，但還沒有到身陷其中無法抽離的地步。我比
  較像個「觀察者」，一直不斷地在觀察事物。

* · 你會不會從以前或當代的其他設計師身上得到靈感？
  都會啊！如果我喜歡他們的作品我就會向他們看
  齊，如果不喜歡我就會想做得比他們更好。

* · 你最喜歡的牌子或人物（可以是任何領域的）以及理
  由？
  沒有。

* · 如果不走設計這一行你會做什麼工作？
  我想我大概會虛度光陰，但説實在的，我不知
  道。

* · 你還會想要挑戰哪一種行業呢？
  我試著不要去想這個問題。我連專注於自己目前
  的工作都很難了！

* · 你的一天大多如何度過？
  一團亂。

How would you describe your style of design?
No idea. How would you describe it?

Are you going to expand your product to a wider range and variety?
As much as I can afford to. The fun is in making the new things. More variety means the opportunity for me to learn new methods and practices, and this is vital for any career.

What's your vision and mission for MISC.?
To be a helping hand in promoting and describing a better way of living together. Reminding people of their responsibilities to others. Using all aspects of design to make things better. Not just faster, higher, bigger or smaller.

What's your best selling design? And why?
'Trust me, cocaine is great. It made me what I am today' A made up quote from George W Bush.

Because it uses the worlds favourite figure of hate and ridicule, it has a drug reference, and it is a strong, simple design.

What's your favourite design? And why?
All of them. They are all my children! LOL.

Since you started your brand, what has been the most joyful thing that has happened to you? And the most difficult?
Meeting people. Not fulfilling its potential.

Do you wear your own designs?
All the time. It's one of the, if not the biggest perk of the job.

Is being a designer a difficult job to handle? How are you feeling being one?
It can be tough, because you're constantly displaying your work, and judging your self on it. However, I don't honestly think of myself as a designer. I occasionally express myself through design, but it's not at a level where I cannot separate myself from it. I'm more of a 'looker'. I'm always looking at things.

Do you draw inspiration from the work of other designers - historic or contemporary?
All of them - if I like their work I want to emulate them. If I don't like their work, I want to better them.

Your favourite brand or character (can be in any category) and the reason?
None.

What would you be doing if you weren't designing?
My fear is that I'd be wasting my time, but, really I don't know.

What other forms of business would you like to venture into one day?
I try not to think about that. I have enough problems concentrating on what I'm currently doing!

What's a typical day like for you?
Messy.

＊・ 對你來說，全世界最能激發你靈感的東西是什麼？
人們的一舉一動。

＊・ 一星期中你最喜愛哪一天？理由為何？
星期天──如果沒工作的話。如果有工作，它仍
會給我前進的動力。它是唯一「每個人」都不用
工作的日子，什麼事也不用做──除非你真的想
找事做。也因此它很美好，讓大家都想找別人共
度。

＊・ 一星期中你最討厭哪一天？理由為何？
此刻，星期五，因為在週末市集交易之前我都無
法放鬆心情。

＊・ 你如何打發時間？
睡覺，觀察事物。

＊・ 你最喜歡的髮型是什麼？
桃樂絲 ² 式的辮子。

＊・ 你的聖典為何？
字典──它能解釋所有的事物──用正確的語言
（不論是什麼語言）。

＊・ 你此刻讀些什麼書？書的內容是什麼？
Caryl Phillips 的《遙遠的海岸》(*A Distant
Shore*)，一本關於人際關係、偏見及人們背負的
包袱的小說。

2 Dorothy，經典電影《綠野仙蹤》的女主角。

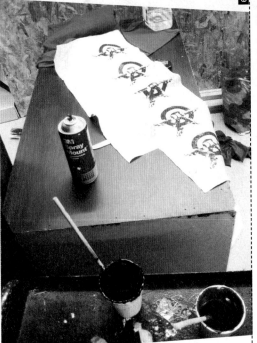

Toby 的印刷工作室

What is the most inspiring thing in the world for you?
The things people do.

What is your favourite day of the week? And why?
Sunday - if I'm off work. If I'm not, then it still gives me something to work toward. It's the only day when almost EVERYONE is off work! No need to do anything unless you really want to, which makes it beautiful that we often want to spend it with each other.

What is your least favourite day of the week? And why?
Right now, Friday, because I still find it hard to relax before the weekend trading.

What do you do to kill time?
Sleep. Look at stuff.

What's your favourite hair style?
Dorothy braids.

What's your bible?
The Dictionary - it helps to explain everything in the right language (whichever that happens to be).

What book are you reading at the moment? And what's it about?
A Distant Shore by Caryl Phillips. A novel about relationships, prejudice, and worldwide personal baggage.

What do you love and hate the most about London?
Exactly that. That London makes it possible to feel such love and hate. In one day you can find so much that is wrong, turn the corner and fall in love. Perhaps it's all the people.

What do you do when you are stuck on a particular design/idea?
Leave it alone or start it again.

How do you handle your stress?
Not as well as I'd like - smart arse answer, I know.

Are you living your ideal lifestyle right now? If not, what's your ideal lifestyle & place to be?
I don't like the thought of a 'lifestyle'.

What keeps you going and stay in tune?
House and Soul and Dreams.

What's your favourite drink, music & film?
Too many of all three - that's why they're all so great, because you can have as many as you like.

＊· 你最喜愛和最討厭倫敦哪一點？
就是這一點！倫敦同時令人又愛又恨，你可以在一天之內經歷一堆不對勁的事，然後轉個身又墜入情網。我想這全都是人的關係吧。

＊· 當工作或思考遇到瓶頸時你都怎麼做？
把它丟在一邊，或重頭開始。

＊· 你如何調適壓力？
調適得不像我希望中那麼好——很圓滑的回答，我知道。

＊· 你現在過的是你夢想中的生活嗎？如果不是，你夢想中的生活型態及地點為何？
我不喜歡「生活型態」這個想法。

＊· 讓你維持生活步調及常規的事物是什麼？
電子樂、靈魂樂和夢想。

＊· 你最喜歡的飲料、音樂類型和電影是什麼？
太多了——這就是它們那麼棒的原因，因為你可以要多少有多少。

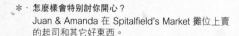

＊‧ 怎麼樣會特別討你開心？
　　Juan & Amanda 在 Spitalfield's Market 攤位上賣
　　的起司和其它好東西。

＊‧ 你都怎麼烹調馬鈴薯？
　　我通常弄成馬鈴薯泥，雖然我的味蕾最近迷上了
　　烘烤口味。馬鈴薯真是個極品！

＊‧ 夢想中的工作是？
　　我現在的工作，但更好的待遇。

＊‧ 什麼是你從沒有嘗試過、但有一天一定會去做的一件
　　事？
　　做個好父親。

＊‧ 最近迷些什麼東西？
　　醒來的感覺。

＊‧ 什麼是你生活中不可或缺的事物？
　　自由，即便只是假象。

＊‧ 請用簡單的一句話來形容你自己。
　　睡、思考、表達、思考。

＊‧ 要不要跟大家分享你的祕密？
　　妳聽了是不會原諒我的。

＊‧ 夢想能……
　　永遠快樂，在一個更加快樂的世界裡……並且，
　　能意識到它。

What would be a special treat for you?
Cheese and other nice stuff from Juan and Amanda at Spitalfields Market.

What's your usual way of cooking potato?
My usual way is mash, although my taste buds have recently opened up to baked and roast potatoes. What a great vegetable!

A dream job to you is...
Mine, but far better paid.

What have you not tried to do, but would definitely want to try one day?
Be a good father.

What is your latest obsession?
Waking up.

What can't you live without?
Freedom, or at least the pretence of it.

Please describe yourself in a short sentence.
Sleep, think, express, think.

Dare to share one of your secrets?
You'd never forgive me ;p

Dream to be...
Happy most of the time, in a world that's happier more of the time... and at least acknowledges it.

Toby 在 Portobello Market 的攤位

K 45
Kazuko Howlin

www.k45design.com
info@k45design.com
sell at selected London boutiques
shop address_such as Junky Styling : 12 Draywalk The Old
Trumans Brewery 91/95 Brick Lane E1 6RF; Beyond the Valley
: 26 Ganton St W1F 7QZ; Boutique SE1 : 8 Stoney St Borough
Market SE1; The Gladys : 253 Portobello rd Notting hill gate
W11 1CR
studio address_No 200 The Triangle 129-131 Mare St London E8
3RH

Kazuko Howlin 在 Spitalfield's Market 的攤位

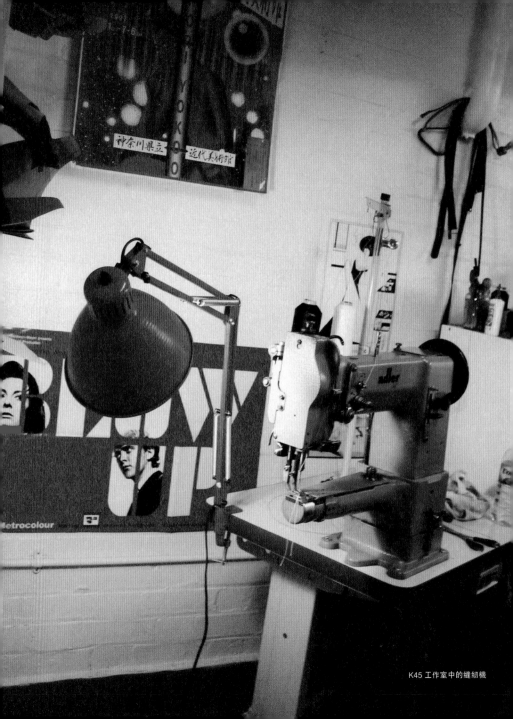

K45 工作室中的縫紉機

Kazuko 最欣賞的 插畫作品

日本高中時期的一堂手工課，引發了 Kazuko 對皮製品的興趣。當時的課題是：自由發揮。跟很多女孩子一樣，Kazuko 喜歡買皮包，所以她選擇了皮革當材料，決定做一個皮背包給自己。看了她當時做的背包照片之後，我一點都不敢相信這是初學者的作品，不得不稱讚她在這方面的潛力！高中畢業之後，Kazuko 來到倫敦就讀倫敦時裝學院 (London College of Fashion) 的飾品配件設計。三年前大學畢業之後，她身體力行了多年來的願望——自創品牌 K45，在倫敦市集中賣起她親手設計製造的背包、皮帶、皮夾等皮製品。

個子雖小，卻總是神采奕奕的 Kazuko，身上彷彿有一股停不下來的節奏。無論在那裡看見她，總是一個大大的笑容問你最近好不好。K45 的產品和她表現出來的態度幾乎沒有衝突點，代表積極的三原色經常被反覆運用在產品中，簡單的幾何圖形線條搭配飽合色彩正是 K45 最吸引人的特色之處。創作靈感來自於 60 年代的時尚，Kazuko 的希望（也是使命）很單純：設計出既耐用又不退流行，會讓你珍惜一輩子的貼身物品。

身為自由創作工作者，Kazuko 每天激勵自己努力工作的祕訣就是走出家門，將工作和住家環境徹底分開。她的工作室，小小一間房卻散發出無比忙碌的氣氛，掛滿了到處搜集而來色彩豐富的布料、皮料和各種工具，亂而有序，有股不斷運轉的活力。她表示自己閒不下來，叫她工作狂或勞碌命都可以，即使工作完畢回到家中她也無法靜靜的坐著休息，一定得找事情做，例如擦地板做家事（她老公真幸福！）。所以她也無法忍受 Spitalfield's Market 2005 年有了變動後明顯的冷清，因此也加速了她對事業前途的不同規劃——離開市集，開始 K45 的另一個階段，佈點販售、改良設計以及找尋更有效率的生產線。

Kazuko 身上停不下來的那股節奏就是她那充沛的精力，跟她聊天可以很清楚地感受到她對生活點滴的珍惜以及存在就是快樂的態度。姑且不論她真正的內心世界是否也和她表現出來的步調一致，可是她樂觀積極的態度對旁觀者而言永遠是啟發。

Kazuko 做的第一個包包

* · 跟我們談談 K45 這個品牌，妳是怎麼想到這個產品名稱及概念的？

品牌是根據我的名字字首「K」以及我的生日四月五日來命名。我是日本人，我們寫生日是先寫月再寫日，我的生日寫法為「4. 5.」，此外，搖滾樂在黑膠唱片的轉動速度是 45 RPM [1]，這也是名稱來源之一。我想將自己與搖滾樂灌注在我的品牌中。

K45 的品牌概念是「每個人都負擔得起的名牌」，目前我正在做限量產品。

* · 妳透過 K45 想表達些什麼？

把 1960 及 70 年代的流行概念融入現代，試著玩出各種色彩元素相結合的可能性。

* · 妳是怎麼將品牌打入市場的？

漸進式的，透過街頭市集 (Street Market) 及各種藝術活動與顧客接觸。此外，我們已經在 Junky Styling、Beyond the Valley、Boutique SE1、及 Gladys 等流行店面販賣我們的產品。

* · 請介紹自己並與大家說說妳的背景。

我是個住在倫敦的日本人，2003 年從倫敦時裝學院 (London College of Fashion) 畢業後創立了我的品牌。然而品牌才開始不久我就必須回去日本，並且在東京重頭開始。一年過後（2004 年 5 月）我和我先生才又回到倫敦，並且終於在倫敦的 Hackney 區讓 K45 這個牌子落地生根。至於我這個人嘛，不喜歡巧克力，喜歡紅酒；橄欖和

紅酒對我來說是個夢幻組合。我對流行品味感覺敏銳，到現在甚至都還會穿我在十六歲時買的上衣和褲子！也因此我希望我的產品對顧客來說也能耐穿耐久。

* · 妳是怎麼開始對時裝與配件有概念並進而產生興趣的？

從小我就對配件很有概念，一點點小裝飾會讓妳顯得獨立、與眾不同。過去我也經常改造自己的東西，不止改造服飾，還改造文具及制服。

* · 妳的產品有哪些種類？還想將觸角伸向何處？

目前產品有很多種類。包括：K45 時尚系列：袋子、皮帶、錢包、袖扣、錢夾；K45 文具系列：萬用手冊、筆套、作品夾；以及 K45 音樂系列：吉他背帶、DJ 袋、設備箱等。我不斷從各種元素中尋找靈感，所以也不知道接下來會創造出什麼產品。

* · 請試著描述妳的工作程序。

我的工作程序很簡單，因為除非有個特別主題，否則我不太常畫畫。我的腦海中總是忽然地出現設計想法，然後我會很快地將它粗略畫下，接著製版、然後開始製作產品。

* · 妳如何推銷並販賣妳的產品？

我們一直在做一些令人興奮的事，像是在東京藝文空間裡的展覽或是在倫敦的市集設攤。K45 不管做什麼事都以創意為主。我們合作的店家都經過精挑細選，它們宣傳 K45 的方式和我們的創意理念能相吻合。

1 RPM = Revolutions Per Minute，黑膠唱片轉動速度。

Tell us a bit about K45. How did you come up with the name and concept?
I named the business using my initial K and my birthday 5th April. I am a Japanese and we write our birthday in order of Month and Date, which mine is 4.5. Also rock'n roll music is spun at 45 RPM. I wanted to connect me and Rock music into my brand.

The concept of K45 is an affordable exclusivity for everyone. I am doing low volume production at the moment.

What are you expressing through K45?
60's 70's taste in modern age. Result of exploring the possibilities of colour combinations.

How did you launch the brand onto the market?
Launched slowly, using street market and arts events to meet customers. We have tried and been retailing at selected boutiques in London such as Junky Styling, Beyond the valley, boutique SE1, and Gladys.

Please introduce yourself & tell us about your background.
I am a Japanese and living in London. After graduated from London College of Fashion in 2003, I started my brand in London. However after I started my business I had to go back to Japan and re-start again in Tokyo and a year later (May 2004) we came back to London and finally K45 Design was settled in Hackney.
About myself, I don't like chocolate, and I love red wine. Olives and Red wine is a magic combination for me. Also my fashion taste is very strong and I am still wearing Tops and Bottoms which I bought when I was 16!! So I hope my creations will last long for my customers.

How did you first become aware of and become interested in fashion & accessories?
I was always aware of accessories since I was small. Because little accents make you different and you will become independent from other people. I used to customise my belongings. Not only fashion wise but also my stationary and school uniforms.

What product range do you have? And what to expand?
We have lots of range right now. Which are:
K45 Fashion : Bag, Belt, Purse, Cuff, Money clip
K45 Stationary : Filo fax, Pen case, Portfolio file.
K45 Music : Guitar strap, DJ bag, Instrument case.
I am always looking for creative inspirations from all elements. So we don't know yet what will be born next.

Please describe your working procedure.
My Creative procedure is very simple, because I don't do much drawing unless there is a theme for it. Designs will come up instantly in my mind and I do rough sketches and start cutting the pattern and then making.

How do you promote and sell your products?
We have been doing lots of exciting things like gallery shows in Tokyo and street markets in London. K45 always wants to be creative in everything we do. The stores that we work with are specially selected because they promote K45 in ways that we appreciate creatively.

K45 工作室

＊・妳身上的必備配件為何？
彩色的亮襪子！

＊・設計師是很難掌握的一個工作嗎？身為一位設計師感想如何？
是的，真的很難，然而這是我夢想中的工作，所以我從不抱怨並且樂在其中。我知道很少人能真正達到他們的目標。

＊・妳會不會從過去或當代其他設計師身上得到靈感？
會呀！皮爾卡登和 YSL 在 60 和 70 年代的設計總是能抓住我的目光。裝飾藝術的圖案和一些插畫家如宇野亞嘉良和橫尾忠也在多方面影響我的設計。

＊・妳最喜歡的牌子或人物（可以是任何領域的）？理由為何？
「日本近江」(Omi Brotherhood)。這是日本一個護唇膏品牌，我已經用了二十年了！我是個沒有護唇膏就活不下去的人，最喜歡薄荷味。

＊・妳對 K45 的期望及目標為何？
製造出可以跟著你一輩子，並且讓你感覺特別的產品。

＊・從妳開始這個品牌作業以來，讓妳最開心的事情是什麼？最難過的呢？
看到人們穿戴或用我的產品的時候最讓我開心。最難過的大概就是缺乏對生意及時尚工業的知識，不過我每天都在學習。

＊・如果不是做設計，妳會考慮做什麼？
也許做一個不知名的藝術家，不過絕對不會是家庭主婦！

What's your vision and mission for K45?
To create things that stay with you for life and make you feel special.

Since you started your brand, what has been the most joyful thing that has happened to you? And the most difficult?
When I saw the people carrying and using my work. That makes me so happy. The most difficult thing is probably a lack of the knowledge of business and fashion industry, however I am learning day by day.

What is a 'must-have' accessory to you?
Colourful and shiny socks!!!!

Is being a designer a difficult job to handle? How are you feeling being one?
Yes it is. However, this is my dream job, so I don't complain and I enjoy it very much. I know that few people get to achieve their ambitions.

Do you draw inspiration from the work of other designers - historic or contemporary?
Yes I do. Pier Cardin and Yves Saint Laurents' designs from the 60's and 70's always catch my eyes. Art deco motif and some illustrators such as Akira Uno and Tadanori Yokoo are always an influence for my design.

Your favourite brand or character (can be in any category) and the reason?
Omi Brotherfood. This is a lip balm company in Japan and I have been using this brand for 20 years! I am a person who can't live without lip balm preferably menthol.

What would you be doing if you weren't designing?
Possibly an unknown fine artist, definitely not house wife though!

What other forms of business would you like to venture into one day?
Interior Furnishings.

London or Tokyo? Why?
Both, I think both cities are very exciting in different ways and I always get inspirations from both. However, being a foreigner in London I often find a difference between the west and east. Everyday discoveries are very exciting and helps for my creation. So it's London with a dash of Tokyo please.

What's a typical day like for you?
Going to studio on my lovely Bike going though London Fields, making new creations at my studio while listening to XFM and having lunch from my favourite Turkish bakery.

＊· 妳還會想要挑戰哪一種行業呢？
室內裝潢。

＊· 倫敦好還是東京好？為什麼？
都好，我覺得這兩個城市令人興奮的地方很不一樣，而我總是能從它們身上分別得到靈感。身為生活在倫敦的外地人，經常能感受到東西方的差異，而每天不同的新發現總是讓我雀躍不已，對我的設計也有很大的幫助。所以應該説我喜歡倫敦和一點點東京的味道吧！

＊· 跟大家描述妳的一天。
騎著我心愛的腳踏車，穿過倫敦的小公園到我的工作室去，在工作室一邊聽 XFM 廣播電台一邊做設計工作，然後到我最愛的土耳其麵包店吃午餐。

K45 工作室

＊・對妳來說，全世界最能激發妳靈感的東西是什麼？
空間。

＊・一星期中妳最喜愛哪一天？理由為何？
星期六，可以整天陪著我老公！

＊・一星期中妳最討厭哪一天？理由為何？
星期天，因為星期一就要來了。

＊・妳如何打發時間？
這陣子我花很多時間上網。

＊・妳的聖典為何？
不算有，不過日本科幻小說家星新一 (Shinichi Hoshi) 是我的最愛，他曾跟我最欣賞的插畫家真鍋博 (Hiroshi Manabe) 合作，星新一[2]的故事配上真鍋博的插畫真是太棒了！

＊・妳此刻讀些什麼書？書的內容是什麼？
我不是個喜歡讀書的人，通常只讀網路或雜誌上的有趣文章，但有時也會讀讀《衛報》The Guardian Newspaper，看來我該開始多讀點書了。不過我是 Manga（日本漫畫）的忠實讀者，是個需要看插圖才讀得下書的人！

＊・妳最喜愛和最討厭倫敦哪一點？
喜歡這裡的人們和被公園與綠地圍繞的感覺，喜歡這裡的運河。討厭倫敦交通。

＊・當工作或思考遇到瓶頸時妳都怎麼做？
做做別的事，試著不要去想它。出去走走總是能讓我頭腦清醒些；跟別人談談、或自己放鬆一下。

＊・妳如何調適妳的壓力？
不去計較太多……或喝喝酒讓自己開心，日本料理也很有幫助。

What is the most inspiring thing in the world for you?
Space.

What is your favourite day of the week? And why?
Saturday. I can spend the time with my husband all day!

What is your least favourite day of the week? And why?
Sunday. Cos Monday is coming tomorrow.

What do you do to kill time?
These days I spend lots of times on internet.

What's your bible?
I don't really like but... Japanese SF writer Shinichi Hoshi is my favourite and he used to work with one of my favourite illustrator called Hiroshi Manabe.
And Shinich's story and Hiroshi's are Magic!!!!

=Shinich Hoshi =
Born in Tokyo on September 6th 1926. Graduated in agricultural chemistry from Tokyo University. After quitting graduate school of Tokyo University, worked for Hoshi Pharmacy Co. His first published story was a short-short 'Sextra' in 1957, and he won Japan Mystery Writers Award by 'Mousou Ginko (Delusion Bank)' in 1968. He is apparently the most copious short-short writer in Japan, who has created more than 1000 titles. Died on December 30th 1997, 18:23 at the age of 71. Some works of his have been translated in various languages, including English. One of his main works is 'Bokko-chan'. His book with Manabe's illustration.

What books are you reading at the moment? And what's it about?
I am not a reading person, I only read interesting articles from the internet or magazines, but I do read the Guardian Newspaper sometimes. I should start reading books more but I was a big Manga reader, so need illustrations to keep me going!!!

What do you love and hate the most about London?
Love about people and am surrounded by lots of green parks and spaces. I love the canals. I hate London transport.

What do you do when you are stuck on a particular design/idea?
Start doing something different and try to not think about it. Going out is always refreshing for my mind. Talking to someone or relaxing by myself.

How do you handle your stress?
Just let it go... or drinking wine will cheer me up. Japanese food helps too.

2 星新一簡介：1926 年 9 月 6 日生於東京，東京大學農化系畢業。東京大學研究所休學後在星製藥廠服務，他第一篇公開發表的作品是 1957 年的極短篇 'Sextra'，1968 年他以《妄想銀行》一書贏得日本推理作家協會賞。他誠然是日本最多產的極短篇小說家，擁有超過一千本的著作。1997 年 12 月 30 日晚上時間 6:23 逝世，享年七十一歲。某些著作譯為多種語言出版。其中一本主要著作為 Bokko-Chan，與插畫家真鍋博合作。

＊．妳現在過的是夢想中的生活嗎？如果不是，妳夢想中
的生活型態及地點為何？
我想住在一幢擁有大花園的房子裡，而且自己動
手裝潢。也想養一隻狗和一隻貓。我會替貓咪取
名字，而我老公 John 負責想狗狗的名字。

＊．讓妳維持生活步調及常規的事物是什麼？
快樂的生活。

＊．妳最喜歡的飲料、音樂類型和電影是什麼？
飲料——我喜歡紅酒、清酒、蘋果汁、日式煎茶
和……再講一次紅酒。
音樂——Primal Scream 樂團、The Stone Roses
樂團、Nick Drake。
電影——《黃色潛水艇》、《發條橘子》
(Clockwork Orange)。

＊．怎麼樣會特別討妳開心？
在倫敦吃壽司——雖然又貴又難吃，但我還是不
能沒有壽司。還有在日本洗溫泉，我喜歡泡澡，
很想念日式泡澡。所以泡個露天溫泉絕對能令我
心花怒放。

＊．妳都怎麼烹調馬鈴薯？
除了做成咖哩，我是不烹調馬鈴薯的，不過我老
公會做。英國人愛死馬鈴薯了！

＊．夢想中的工作是？
我現在的工作，不過必須賺更多錢！

＊．妳從沒有嘗試過、但有一天一定會去做的一件事？
戒煙。

＊．最近迷些什麼東西？
紫色和葡萄。

＊．什麼是妳生活中不可或缺的？
我老公、護唇膏和米飯。

＊．請用簡單的一句話來形容自己。
非常笨手笨腳、有點健忘，腦袋瓜子永遠轉個不
停，情緒化、有些怪里怪氣，是個有創意，開心
的人。

＊．要不要跟大家分享妳的祕密？
咱們去喝一杯時我再告訴你。

＊．夢想能……
舒適度日。

K45 產品

Are you living your ideal lifestyle right now? If not, what's your ideal lifestyle & place to be?
I love to live in spacious house with big garden and want to decorate it by myself one day. I would also love to have a dog and cat. I will name the cat and John will name the dog.

What keeps you going and stay in tune?
Happy life.

What's your favourite drink, music & film?
Drink - I love red wine, sake, apple juice, Japanese green tea and red wine again please.
Music - Primal Scream , The Stone Roses, Nick Drake.
Film - Yellow submarine, Clockwork Orange.

What would be a special treat for you?
Eating Sushi in London. Although it is expensive and not good quality, I can't live without Sushi. Having a Spring bath in Japan, I love having a bath and I do miss Japanese style bath. So, having a bath in the big spring bath in nature will be my big treat.

What's your usual way of cooking potato?
I don't cook potatoes except in curry but my husband does, English people love potatoes!

A dream job to you is...
The job I have now. But I need to earn more money!

What have you not tried to do, but would definitely want to try one day?
Stop smoking.

What is your latest obsession?
Purple colour and grapes.

What can't you live without?
My husband, lip balm, rice.

Please describe yourself in a short sentence.
I am very clumsy. I am a little bit forgetful, having always a busy mind, emotional, little bit eccentric. Creative and happy person.

Dare to share one of your secrets?
I will tell you when we drink together.

Dream to be...
Comfy.

Whim Wham

James (Casey) Jones & Jenny White

info@whimwham.co.uk
sell at Sunday Spitalfield's Market

Jenny 和 James 在他們花園的工具室中工作

Whim Wham 的別針小飾品

開了兩個半小時的車程來到劍橋 (Cambridge) 的一個小鎮拜訪 James 和 Jenny。記得第一次在 Up Market 看到他們,就被他們自製小飾品的懷舊俏皮,和甜美樸實的氣質吸引,所以再遠也值得跑這一趟旅程。抵達之後,驚喜的看見他們準備了滿滿一桌的三明治和漂亮的點心招待我們(我媽媽那天決定跟我一起去,看看我平常到底都在忙些什麼)。如此的備受禮遇在我訪問了這麼多人以來可是頭一遭,我們悠閒的坐下來開始閒聊,暫時告別倫敦匆忙的生活步調……

三年前 James 和 Jenny 自大學畢業,像很多初出茅廬的社會新鮮人一樣滿懷大志的跑到倫敦積極尋找設計工作。但激烈的競爭環境和面對大都市生活的不適應,讓兩人決定返回寧靜規律的小鎮生活。James 為了生活開始了全職郵差的工作,Jenny 則偶爾充當娛母。在這看起來再平凡也不過的生活之下,兩個人卻才華洋溢,對所學所愛的藝術、設計充滿憧憬。他們從來沒有淡忘過他們擁有的藝術創作背景和天份,在平淡的工作之餘也藉由不同的方式來抒發創意靈感。Jenny 會作畫、會做做小東西,而 James 喜歡創作模型。看過 James 大學的作品集之後,我真的對他的一雙巧手配服得五體投地。他告訴我郵差只是過渡時期的工作,希望能多存一點錢投資在作品上。

他真正的希望是能為電影場景製作模型,而這段期間他也不斷塑作不同模型,增加作品的完整性。

他們的品牌 WHIM-WHAM 的起源則是個巧合:有一天 James 在工作坊中隨手畫了一隻木頭鳥,將它切割上漆後拿給 Jenny 看。一直有搜集古董飾品、別針的 Jenny 看了非常喜歡,直覺可以將它做成一只可愛胸針來賣,而同時也意識到這也是個能將他們創意結合的好時機。從那天開始兩個人的生活彷彿有了新的重心,他們到處採集材料,做出各式各樣圖案的木頭胸針、項鍊和機器人鑰匙圈,每個星期天凌晨四點就起床,搭火車到倫敦的市集擺攤。

James 和 Jenny 有著隨和恬淡的生活觀,由他們手工質感的作品中釋放出的那股純樸又懷舊的童稚感和單純的訊息,和他們的生活和個性相互呼應。跟他們聊天之後我心中的想法產生了兩極化,感嘆他們的才華應該得到更多的發揮和延續,不應該被平凡的生活埋沒;但又覺得如果他們能夠從單純生活的點滴中得到驚喜與滿足,也是另一種創作靈感的啟發吧!就像 Jenny 所說的:朝著夢想前進的過程如履薄冰,但每前進一小步都會得到一大步的成就感,這種感覺也許會比住在夢想之中來的踏實。

＊‧ 請跟我們談談 WHIM WHAM，你們是如何想出這個
名稱及整個產品概念的？

WHIM WHAM 這個牌子是關於對色彩單純的愛，
穿戴讓自己會心一笑，如扣子般可愛的，如回溯
過往時光般甜蜜的小飾品，我們用心、用愛來製
作這些小飾品。它們可愛、迷人，有點1950 年
代那種很女生的漂亮風格。WHIM WHAM 這個名
字就是在表達這些東西。

＊‧ 你們透過 WHIM WHAM 想跟大家表達些什麼？
我們對媚俗藝術的熱愛，及與童年夢想緊密的結
合。

＊‧ 你們是如何將這個品牌打入市場的？
2005 年 1 月份時在 Truman Brewery 的 Up
Market 弄了個攤位。事實上我們也沒有正式的去
打入什麼市場，只不過到那裡、把產品擺設好，
然後等著看會有什麼結果而已。

＊‧ 請各自介紹一下自己並告訴大家你們的背景。
Jenny　我們在就讀藝術學院一年級時認識，然後
就一直在一起了，James 主修雕塑，我主修織
品。畢業後我們各自嘗試過各種不同的工作，但
發現還是跟對方在一起時最快樂，所以兩人一起
做個可以把各自專長融入的工作似乎成了最自然
的一件事……

＊‧ 你們是怎麼開始注意到時裝與配件工業，並進而對它
產生興趣的？
James　Jenny 一直都很愛好珠寶，她有收集古典
胸針與項鍊的嗜好。我們曾經跑遍各地去找這些
東西：包括車庫拍賣、慈善商店、古董店和跳蚤
市場等，如果我有事去別的城鎮工作也會為她帶
回來一些。所以這是她一直愛好的事，而我也因
為她而變得很感興趣。

有一天我在工具室混時，隨手畫了隻鳥在木頭
上，將它切下來、雕刻、上漆，然後拿給 Jenny
看。她看了很喜歡，我們也認為可以將它做成
一只很棒的胸針。剎那間我們腦中突然有了個想
法──這不就是我們一直在尋找的，能結合我們
兩人專長和嗜好的辦法嗎！另一個好處是，飾品
配件運輸容易，方便我們將它們帶到倫敦市集去
賣給更多人。

＊ 你們的產品有哪些種類？還想將觸角伸向何處？
用樺木和桃心木做的項鍊、鑰匙圈、包包吊牌
和胸針，打上高分子蠟 (Carnuba Wax) 或彩釉
上色，再用緞帶、金銀絲線、古董人造寶石或
Swarovski 的水晶加以裝飾。我們計劃製造一些
依照比例放大的胸針，可以將它們像美麗的雕像
般掛在牆上。

＊ 跟大家説説你們的工作程序。
我們做這些東西做得很快樂。

＊ 你們如何推銷並販賣你們的產品？
現階段我們每個星期五和星期天在 Spitalfield's
Market 販賣我們的產品，但我們希望很快能拓展
到其它市集。由於我們算是初涉此行業，所以也
沒有做太多的宣傳，在開始做之前我們並沒有真
正了解到必須要考慮的事情這麼多。不過目前我
們每賣出一樣東西，總是會在顧客的袋子裡放一
些小驚喜給他們，如一支棒棒糖、或近來常放的
小徽章等。等他們回家打開袋子時會看到袋子中
多出一樣小禮物，希望如此一來 WHIM WHAM
這個牌子會在他們腦海裡生根，進而跟他們的朋
友提起我們。

＊ 你們對 WHIM WHAM 的期望及目標為何？
我們希望 WHIM WHAM 成為一個國際性的品
牌，並且在看到人們戴著我們產品時會説：
「哇！你好 WHIM WHAM 哦！」我們希望能成
為配件界的 Cath Kidston [1]。最大的希望是能有
一間自己的店，除了賣 WHIM WHAM 珠寶及配
件外還能賣 WHIM WHAM 時裝、居家飾品及室
內裝潢系列等。但身為新面孔，我們計劃要製作
更多的產品種類，並花更多時間在宣傳品牌、建
立專屬網站及從目前的後花園工具室搬到一間正
式的工作室。

1 英國著名居家品牌，以色彩豐富多變著稱。

Tell us a bit about WHIM WHAM. How did you
come up with the name and concept?
WHIM WHAM is about a childlike love of colour,
wearing things that make you smile, that are cute as a
button, sweetly retro, handmade with a lot of love and
care, extremely endearing, very charming, and with
kind of a 1950's girlish prettiness. The name WHIM
WHAM express's all of this.

What are you expressing through WHIM WHAM?
Our love of the kitsch experience and a strong
connection to the idealism of our childhoods.

How did you launch the brand onto the market?
In January 2005 with a stall at Upmarket at the Truman
Brewery. We didn't exactly launch our brand onto the
market, we just turned up, set up our stall and waited
to see what happened.

Please introduce yourself & tell us about your
background.
Jenny We met in our first year at Art college and have
been together ever since. James studied sculpture and
I studied fine art textiles. After we graduated we both
tried lots of different things but what we enjoyed most
was spending time together so it seemed a natural way
to do something together that we could feed both our
skills into...

How did you first become aware of and become
interested in fashion & accessories?
Jenny has always loved jewellery, she has a collection
of vintage brooches and necklaces, and we used to
go all over the place looking for them, car boot sales,
charity shops, antiques markets and flea markets.
I'd often bring pieces back for her if I'd been working in
a different town for the day. So it was something she
always had a love of and I had an interest in through
her. Then I was fiddling about in the shed one day and
drew a bird on a piece of wood, cut it out, carved it and
painted it, and took it to show Jenny, she really liked it
and we realised it would make a great brooch.
A light bulb went on in our heads and we realised that
this was the creative outlet for our skills and interests
that we had been looking for. The other bonus was
that jewellery and accessories are something that
could be transported easily to the wide audience at the
London fashion markets.

What product range do you have? And what to
expand?
Necklaces, keyrings, bag charms and brooches, made
from mahogany and birch wood, polished with carnuba
wax or painted with brightly coloured enamels and
embellished with satin ribbon, gold and silver findings,
vintage diamante, and swarovski crystals. We plan to
make scaled up versions of our brooches that can be
hung on the wall like a pretty sculpture.

Please describe your working procedure.
We have fun making things.

How do you promote and sell your products?
At the moment we sell at Spitalfields Market on Fridays
and Sundays but we hope to add other markets soon.
As we are still very new at this we haven't really done
much promotion, we never realised just how much
there is to think about before we started. One thing we
have done though is when people buy something, we
always give them a little surprise in the bag with the
item, like a lollypop or lately we've been putting in little
badges, so that when they get home and open the bag,
they find an extra little present and hopefully that will
make WHIM WHAM stick in their mind and they'll tell
their friends about us.

What's your vision and mission for WHIM WHAM?
We'd like WHIM WHAM to become a world wide brand,
for people to see someone wearing our pieces and say
'oh that's so WHIM WHAM '.
We'd like to be seen as the Cath Kidston of the
accessories world. Ultimately we'd like to have our
own boutique selling WHIM WHAM jewellery and
accessories as well as WHIM WHAM clothing and
WHIM WHAM homes and interiors. But for starters
we plan to keep building up our product range, devote
more time to promoting whim wham, set up a website
and move from our garden shed to a proper studio.

臥室牆上的畫作是 Jenny 的作品

＊‧ 從你們開始這個品牌作業以來，讓你們感到最開心的
事情是什麼？最難過的呢？
最開心的是我們賣出第一件產品的時刻，最難過
的是屏息等待那一刻的時候。

＊‧ 你們有做其它工作嗎？
James 有的，我是個全職郵差。
Jenny 沒有，我現在把全副心力放在 WHIM
WHAM 上，但偶爾會兼職做做保姆。

＊‧ 跟對方一起工作的感覺是什麼？
James 跟一個想法相同的人一起工作是件很棒的
事，但想法太接近有時也會起爭執。
Jenny 我從不想跟其他人一起工作，很多時候我
們會同時想出一模一樣的點子，我想我們的腦波
頻率大概是一樣的吧！比較討厭的地方是我們相
處出現問題時會影響到 WHIM WHAM 的作業，
反之亦然。

＊‧ 什麼是你們的「必備配件」？
James 新奇的鑰匙圈。
Jenny 任何能使穿戴者及看到他們的人會心一笑
的東西。

＊‧ 你們會不會從以前或當代的其他設計師身上得到靈
感？
James 我從兒童雜誌、童書的插畫，及我自己的
童年記憶上得到靈感。
Jenny 基本上我發現閱讀《愛麗絲夢遊仙境》或
格林童話一類的書，會比其他設計師的作品更能
激發我的靈感。

＊‧ 你們最喜愛的品牌或人物（可以是任何領域的）以及
理由？
James 英國本地的速食店「美國雞」(U.S.A.
Chicken)，他們的薯條很好吃。
Jenny 日本三麗鷗 (Sanrio)，特別是雙子星系列
(Twin Stars)。

＊‧ 如果不是做這行你們會從事什麼工作？
James 跟 Jenny 一起賣玩具。
Jenny 跟 James 做些別的什麼。

＊‧ 你們還會想要挑戰哪一種行業呢？
James 我想要擁有一間糖果店。
Jenny 我想編寫和製作自己的動畫片。

＊‧ 跟大家描述你們的一天。
James 早起，走來走去，再走來走去，吃東西，
然後走到花園的工具室開始做東西。
Jenny 起床，到花園盡頭的工具室去開暖氣，在
工具室解凍的同時回來沖個澡並喝幾杯茶，再回
工具室去，開始把 James 前一晚切割好的東西加
以細畫與雕刻，約六小時後上去我們的辦公室兼
臥室，訂購缺少的材料、裝飾任何待以裝飾的產
品，然後再回到工具室一直工作到晚餐時間。晚
餐後我會坐在桌前做項鍊，在筆記上亂畫，寫下
一些粗略的想法，直到就寢。

＊‧ 對你們來說，全世界最能激發你們靈感的東西是什
麼？
James 我的最佳拍檔 Jenny。
Jenny 我的姪子姪女。

Since you started your brand, what has been the most joyful thing that has happened to you? And the most difficult?

The most joyful thing was when we sold our first piece. The most difficult was holding our breath and waiting for that sale.

Do you have any other job?

James   Yes, I am a full time postman.

Jenny   No, at the moment I'm devoting myself to WHIM WHAM. But I work as a childrens nanny now and then.

What is it like to work with each other? (the happiest and most painful moments)

James   It is great to work with someone who is on my wavelength. Sometimes our similarities result in an ideas clash.

Jenny   There is no one else I'd rather work. A lot of the time we'll each come up exactly the same idea at the same time - I guess our brains must work on the same frequency. The hard part is if we're having a problem in our relationship it spills over into whimwham time and vice versa.

What is a 'must-have' accessory to you?

James   Novelty keyring.

Jenny   Anything that makes the wearer and the people they meet smile.

Do you draw inspiration from the work of other designers - historic or contemporary?

James   I get inspired by illustrations from childrens magazines, books and memories of my own childhood.

Jenny   Generally I find reading books like Alice In Wonderland and Grimms Fairy Tales more inspirational than the work of other designers.

Your favourite brand or character (can be in any category) and the reason?

James   My local fast food restaurant -USA Chicken. They make a mean french frie.

Jenny   Sanrio. In particular The Little Twin stars.

What would you be doing if you weren't doing this?

James   Selling vintage toys with Jenny.

Jenny   Something else with James.

What other forms of business would you like to venture into one day?

James   I would like to own a sweet shop.

Jenny   I'd like to write and produce my own animated feature film.

What's a typical day like for you?

James   Early start. Walking. Walking some more. Eat. Go to my shed to get making.

Jenny   Get up. Go out to our shed at the bottom the garden and turn the heater on. Go back in have a shower and several cups of tea while the shed defrosts. Go out to the shed and start sanding and carving the pieces that James has cut out the night before, after about six hours go up to our office/bedroom and place orders for any materials we are low on. Add decoration to any pieces that are ready for decorating. Then go back out to the shed until dinnertime. After dinner sit at my desk making necklaces or doodling in my notebook and scribbling down ideas until bedtime.

What is the most inspiring thing in the world for you?

James   My partner in crime jenny.

Jenny   My niece and nephew.

兩人的臥室

工具室中的小東西

* · 一星期中你們最喜愛哪一天？理由為何？

    James 任何可以讓我在太陽昇起後還能賴在床上繼續睡的日子。

    Jenny 星期三，我喜歡身在一週正中間一日的感覺，半週過去了但還有半週留著。

* · 一星期中你們最討厭哪一天？理由為何？

    James 星期一，我上一週的精神都還沒有恢復過來。

    Jenny 星期一，James 還沒從上一週的精神恢復過來所以脾氣很差。

* · 你們如何打發時間？

    James 我沒時間可以打發。

    Jenny eBay 是世上最能打發時間的靈藥，在 eBay 上頭隨便逛一下就可以打發好幾個鐘頭的時間。

* · 你們的聖典為何？

    James 《星際大戰玩具指南》(Star Wars: the Action Figure Archive)。

    Jenny Vogue 雜誌。

＊‧你們此刻讀些什麼書？書的內容是什麼？

James 工具目錄，一本關於工具的書。

Jenny 我在讀芙列達‧卡蘿 (Frida Kahlo)的傳記，她是我最喜歡的藝術家之一，如妳所能預期，這本書全是關於她的事蹟。

＊‧你們最喜愛和最討厭倫敦哪一點？

James 我喜歡它能讓我買到各式各樣的東西，但倫敦很髒，總是讓我想泡澡。

Jenny 喜歡：維多利亞與亞伯特博物館 (The Victoria and Albert Museum)；討厭：污染。

＊‧當工作或思考遇到瓶頸時你們都怎麼做？

James 討論、煩躁、製作、討論、必要的話再重新製作，然後找到解決之道。

Jenny 我們會互相轟炸彼此的腦袋直到「打通」思路為止，其間總是有大吵大鬧的情況，不過當找到解決之道並順利設計出來後，我們總是會給對方一個擁抱。

＊‧你們如何應付壓力？

James 大啖蛋糕和烤餅。

Jenny 對 James 大吼大叫和吃巧克力。

＊‧你們現在過的是夢想中的生活嗎？如果不是，你們夢想中的生活型態及地點為何？

James 我不認為世上有任何地方能接近所謂的「理想」，不過我蠻想有自己的家庭和孩子的。

Jenny 擁有夢想中的生活一點也不好玩，比較好玩的是你努力達到夢想的過程，並且經歷一場冒險。只要我們擁有彼此，有間可以遮風避雨之地，其它的一切都算是恩典。

＊‧讓你們維持生活步調及常規的事物是什麼？

James 對彼此的信念。誠實。

Jenny 家人的支持；及擁有 James 讓我笑口常開。

＊‧你們最喜歡的飲料、音樂類型和電影是什麼？

James 茶；貓王的專輯佔了我收藏的大多數；《魔王迷宮》(The Labyrinth) 第一集，它的魔力讓我百看不厭。

Jenny 蘋果汁；鮑布‧狄倫 (Bob Dylan)；《魔王迷宮》。

What is your favourite day of the week? And why?
James Any day that enables me to stay in bed after the sun has come up.
Jenny Wednesday. I like the feeling of being in the middle of the week. Half of the week has gone but theres still half the week left.

What is your least favourite day of the week? And why?
James Monday - I haven't gotten over the week before.
Jenny Monday - James hasn't gotten over the week before and is a grumpy guts all day.

What do you do to kill time?
James I don't have any to kill.
Jenny eBay is the greatest time killer in the world. Hours can disappear in a flash when looking on eBay.

What's your bible?
James *The Star Wars 'Action Figure Archive'.*
Jenny *Vogue* magazine.

What book are you reading at the moment? And what's it about?
James A tools catalogue. It is about tools.
Jenny I'm reading a biography of Frida Kahlo. She's one of my favourite artists - and as you might expect it's all about Frida Kahlo.

What do you love and hate the most about London?
James I love it's eclectic mix of shopping. But I always feel it makes me want to take a bath.
Jenny Love - The Victoria and Albert Museum. Hate- the pollution.

What do you do when you are stuck on a particular design/idea?
James Discuss, fret, make, discuss, remake if necessary and reach a solution.
Jenny We bang our heads together until we get 'unstuck' on the idea. There's usually some shouting involved from both of us but always a hug when we finally sort the design out.

How do you handle your stress?
James Eating cakes and pastries.
Jenny Shout at James and eat chocolate.

Are you living your ideal lifestyle right now? If not, what's your ideal lifestyle & place to be?
James I don't think there is anything quite like ideal. But I would like to own my own home and have children.
Jenny Theres no fun in having the ideal, it's much more fun trying to get there, and having one big adventure. As long as we've got each other and a roof over our heads anything else is a bonus.

What keeps you going and stay in tune?
James Faith in ourselves. Honesty.
Jenny The support of my family. Having James to make me laugh.

What's your favourite drink, music & film?
James Tea. Elvis is abundant amongst my music collection. *Labyrinth* - I never tire of it's magic.
Jenny Apple juice. Bob Dylan. *Labyrinth*

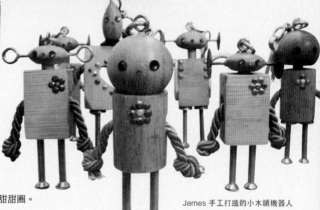

James 手工打造的小木頭機器人

＊‧怎麼樣會特別討你們開心？
James 到海邊去，在沙灘上大吃熱甜甜圈。
Jenny 招待我到美容院。

＊‧你們通常都怎麼調烹馬鈴薯？
James 薯條。
Jenny 先煮沸，再跟蔬菜香腸一起磨成馬鈴薯泥。

＊‧夢想中的工作是？
James 可以用我的點子賺大錢的工作。
Jenny 在我最好的搭檔及朋友身邊做創意工作。

＊‧什麼是你們從沒有嘗試過、但有一天一定會去做的一件事？
James 學開車。
Jenny 生個小寶寶。

＊‧最近迷些什麼東西？
James 我的 BMX 自行車，雖然它現在還不能騎。
Jenny 健達 ² 的快樂河馬系列 (Kinder Happy Hippo)。

＊‧什麼是你們生活中不可或缺的？
James 有一間超級市場自己製作的便宜瑞士巧克力捲。
Jenny 健達快樂河馬系列。

＊‧請你們用簡單的一句話來形容自己。
James 彼得潘真人版，一個小孩的靈魂被困在大人軀體裡。
Jenny 一個富有哲學思維的小精靈。

＊‧要不要跟大家分享你們的祕密？
James 我其實蠻喜歡吃扇貝配醋的，但它們會讓我口臭。
Jenny 我的左耳跟小精靈的耳朵很像（有點尖）。

＊‧夢想能……
James 成為最好的。
Jenny 在墨西哥。

2 Kinder，著名巧克力品牌，「健達出奇蛋」為其代表。

What would be a special treat for you?
James   Going to the seaside and eating hot doughnuts on the beach.
Jenny   Going to the beauty parlour.

What's your usual way of cooking potato?
James   In chip format.
Jenny   Boiled and mashed with veggie sausages stuck in it.

A dream job to you is...
James   One that allows me to use my creative juices to make big bucks.
Jenny   One that allows me to work creatively alongside my partner and best friend.

What have you not tried to do, but would definitely want to try one day?
James   Learn to drive.
Jenny   Have a baby.

What is your latest obsession?
James   My BMX bike, although it is still unrideable.
Jenny   Kinder Happy Hippos.

What can't you live without?
James   A particular supermarket's own brand of chocolate economy swiss roll.
Jenny   Kinder Happy Hippos.

Please describe yourself in a short sentence.
James   A Peter Pan figure. A boy trapped in a man's body.
Jenny   A philosophical little pixie.

Dare to share one of your secrets?
James   I am quite partial to cockles in vinegar, but they tend to make my breath smell.
Jenny   My left ear is very like the ear of a pixie (slightly pointy).

Dream to be...
James   The best.
Jenny   In Mexico.

Jenny 的古典別針收藏

snuglo

Lisa Quinn

www.Snuglo.com
info@Snuglo.com
sell online trough the website and at shops worldwide
shop address_ WWW.SNUGLO.COM
studio address_ Unit 1c 1st Floor Highgate Business Centre 33,
Greenwood Place, London NW5 11B

more fore-shorten
or flatter t

在成人的世界裡，T恤上的標語是一種全方位的溝通藝術——它不但表達出設計師或藝術家最直接的自我；也反應出穿著者的品味、個性、幽默感和想法；它是意識形態的表現工具，是軟性的政治訴求，更是「現在流行什麼」的評量標準之一。

在寶寶的世界裡，雖然沒有牽扯到如此複雜的層面，可是可想而知的是他們也有很多要說的話，只是無法用言語表達；這幾年來在大人的幫助之下，嬰兒標語T恤在英國大行其道，漸漸走出了一套寶寶流行指標。

當今市面上數不清的嬰兒標語T恤品牌中，Lisa 於1999 年創始的 SNUGLO 可說是其中比較出色的品牌之一，在很多大型百貨公司或小店都可以看見 SNUGLO 的小衣服小帽子。產品的特色很一致：簡短可愛的句子配上色彩清晰飽合的印刷圖像，幽默、簡單、搶眼。Lisa 表示，當初會想出這個點子是因為原本是想設計一份特別的禮物送給她好朋友的新生兒，但自認在圖像設計方面能力的不足，於是她想出了一些和嬰兒有關的可愛、調皮句子，改以文字來表達，印刷在嬰兒T恤上面。結果禮物呈現出來的溫馨逗趣深受朋友的喜愛，進而鼓舞 Lisa 創造了 SNUGLO。

她開心的說起許多明星、名人都曾為他們的小孩購買 SNUGLO 的產品，並且穿著 SNUGLO 拍過很多雜誌；令她最興奮的一張照片是裘德洛 (Jude Law) 和他的小孩玩耍的照片。照片中裘德洛的小孩穿著 Lisa 賣得最好的經典作品 'I WANT CHIPS CHOCOLATE AND CAKE'（我要薯條巧克力和蛋糕）；更有趣的是，也有很多媽媽們跟 Lisa 反應說這其實也正是她們的心聲，所以大人的衣服也成了 Lisa 計劃開發的系列之一。我想如果看見媽媽和寶寶一起穿著 'I WANT CHIPS CHOCOLATE AND CAKE' 的衣服一起出現，一定是可愛又有趣的畫面。

到了 2005 年 SNUGLO 就已經六歲了，在眾多競爭對手和英國零售業不景氣的情況之下，還是持續成長。從六年前每個星期自己跑市集做生意，到現在全國都有銷售點，市集的攤位則交由別人經營；有工作室、助手，並請設計公司替她完稿、製做網站，還定期參加商展，成功地創造了這個品牌。Lisa 對於自己的事業仍有許多遠景和堅持：除了保持產品的質感和特色，她堅持所有 SNUGLO 生產線都留在英國，以行動來支持平等交易和英國本土製造業。已經是兩個孩子的媽媽的她，更是無法接受有些第三世界國家使用幼小童工的不人道行為。

回想起創業過程，Lisa 仍然有感而發地說：「所有設計師都會面臨到什麼都得自己來的艱辛過程，唯一能做的就是硬著頭皮一步一步去做，堅持你認為對的事，並學習在組織自己當中找到平衡點。」

＊・跟我們談談 SNUGLO，妳是怎麼想到這個名稱及整個產品概念的？

SNUGLO 是個酷酷的，針對零至八歲兒童設計的服飾品牌，有可愛聰明的原創設計和特出的色彩運用。我會想到 SNUGLO 這個名稱是因為在這之前是做一些有趣又輕軟的嬰兒用毛毯子和鞋子，點綴上兼備安全性又有設計感的發亮貼布。這個名字結合了 Snug（舒適的）──因為羊毛是這麼的柔軟且舒適，及 glo（發亮）──指那些會發亮的布料──這兩個字。SNUGLO 將會再次推出軟毛搭配發亮材質的系列有趣設計。

＊・妳透過 SNUGLO 想跟大家表達些什麼？

透過 SNUGLO 我想表現我的設計概念，以及當我還是個孩子時所希望的穿著打扮方式，1970 年代的兒童服飾可沒那麼好看。

＊・妳設計寶寶 T 恤時最喜愛用的主題是什麼？

強烈的圖像、巧妙結合各種色彩的詼諧語彙。

＊・妳是如何開始以這個牌子打入市場的？

我起步於倫敦的 Spitalfield's Market，在那裡我供應產品給一些店家，後來成立了 www.snuglo.com 的網路商店。

＊・請介紹一下自己並告訴我們妳的背景。

我叫 Lisa Quinn，愛爾蘭人。一直都對設計和時尚很感興趣。我離開校園後曾在愛爾蘭 Kilkenny 郡 Thomastown 的 Grennan Mill Craft School 修了一年的藝術及工藝基礎課程，緊接著取得都柏林 The Grafton Academy of Dress Designing 的時尚設計證書。1995 年搬來倫敦，1999 年成立 SNUGLO 品牌。

Tell us a bit about SNUGLO. How did you come up with the name and concept?
SNUGLO is an über cool range of clothing for little people from 0-8 yrs. Original cute and witty designs incorporating SNUGLO 's trademark use of colour.
I came up with the name SNUGLO as originally I did fun and fluffy fleece baby blankets, hoodies and booties combined with applique reflective fabric as both a safety and design feature. The name SNUGLO is a combination of the word snug (as the fleece was so soft and snuggly) and the word glo (as the reflective fabric). SNUGLO will be re-launching its fun fleece + reflective range soon.

What are you expressing through SNUGLO?
Through SNUGLO I am expressing my design ideas and how I wish I had been dressed as a child.
The children's clothing available in the 70's wasn't that nice.

What's your favourite themes for the baby t-shirts?
Strong graphic, witty slogans using great colour combinations.

How did you launch the brand onto the market?
I started through Spitlefields Market in London, from there I supplied shops and then established www.Snuglo.com the online shop.

Please introduce yourself & tell us about your background.
My name is Lisa Quinn and I'm from Ireland. I have always been interested in design and fashion.
When I left school I did a 1 year foundation course in art and craft at 'Grennan Mill', Thomastown, Co. Kilkenny, Ireland. This was followed by a diploma in fashion design from 'The Grafton Academy' Dublin. I moved to London in 1995 and established SNUGLO in 1999.

Funky fashion babywear available online at **www.snuglo.com**

Jude Law 的孩子（中間）穿著SNUGLO的衣服

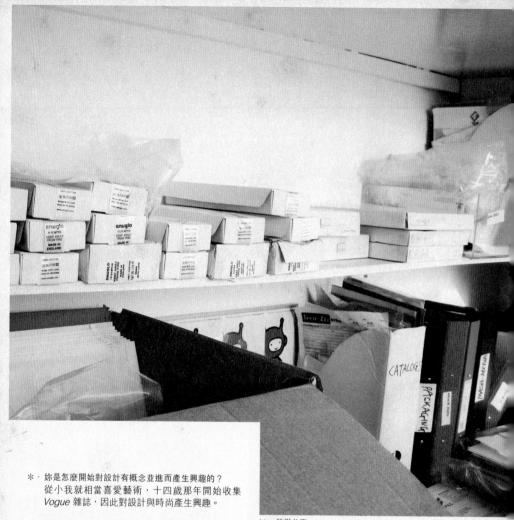

Lisa 的辦公室

＊‧妳是怎麼開始對設計有概念並進而產生興趣的？
　　從小我就相當喜愛藝術，十四歲那年開始收集
　　Vogue 雜誌，因此對設計與時尚產生興趣。

＊‧請描述妳的工作程序。
　　任何事物都可以激發我的靈感──色彩、旅行、
　　現代文化、食物、人、城市、雜誌、電影、電
　　視。

＊‧妳會將產品擴展至更廣的範圍與更多種類嗎？
　　會的，我將服飾年齡層提高到八歲兒童，也開始
　　設計女性T恤，並且開發各種產品、材質及玩具
　　等。

＊‧妳如何推銷並販賣妳的產品？
　　透過媒體和公關、商展及廣告。

＊‧妳對 SNUGLO 的期望及目標為何？
　　我的期望是創造一個維持高格調設計及色彩
　　運用的強勢品牌，並且在英國製造生產。因為
　　SNUGLO 相信公平交易、本土製造生產、最低基
　　本工資及公平的勞動行為。當然 SNUGLO 的希
　　望是產品能讓你會心一笑！

一包一包的庫存

How did you first become aware of and interested in design?
I always loved art from when I was very young. I became interested in design and fashion aged about 14, when I started collecting *Vogue* magazines.

Please describe your working procedure.
I am inspired by everything - colours, travel, modern culture, food, people, cities, magazines, films, TV.

Are you going to expand your products to a wider range and variety?
Yes I am expanding our kids clothing range up to 8 years, introducing women's t-shirts and developing different products, materials, toys etc.

How do you promote and sell your products?
Through press and pr, trade shows and advertising.

What's your vision and mission for SNUGLO?
My vision is to create a really strong brand whilst maintaining a high standard of design and use of colour and to manufacture in England, as SNUGLO believes in fair trade, local manufacture, minimum wages and fair labour practice. Above all SNUGLO wants to make you smile!

What's your best selling design? And why?
'Want chips chocolate and cake', I think because it is a universal thing true of both children and adults, also the colours used for this design work very well. Blue print with chocolate brown or pink print with chocolate brown.

Since you started your brand, what has been the most joyful thing that has happened to you? And the most difficult?
→The most joyful thing is to have established a successful company and have people love my designs. The most difficult is being away from my two little girls Eva and Georgia.

What do you think of the baby-fashion nowadays?
It is getting better, it used to be quite conservative, with limited choice and colour. It's now a very cool / up and coming industry.

Is being a designer a difficult job to handle? How are you feeling being a designer?
I don't find being a designer that difficult, but combined with motherhood and being a business women, very difficult.

Do you draw inspiration from the work of other designers - historic or contemporary?
Yes! Who doesn't?

＊·妳賣得最好的設計是什麼？原因為何？
「我要薯條、巧克力和蛋糕」這個設計。我想是因為這句話道出了世界上許多大人和小孩共同的心聲，此外藍色搭配巧克力色或粉紅色搭配巧克力色的色彩運用得宜也是它成功的因素之一。

＊·從這個品牌開始運作以來，讓妳最感到開心的事情是什麼？最難過的呢？
最開心的是我成立了一間成功的公司，同時有人喜愛我的設計。最難過的是必須跟我兩個小女兒Eva 和 Georgia 分隔兩地時。

＊·妳對現今的嬰幼兒服飾業感想如何？
愈來愈好了，它曾經很保守，色彩和選擇性都很少，現在成了個很酷的新興產業。

＊·設計師是很難掌握的一個工作嗎？身為一位設計師感覺如何？
當一名設計師並不難，但要同時兼顧一個好母親與職業婦女的角色就非常難了。

＊·妳會不會從過去或當代的藝術家或設計師身上得到靈感？
會啊！誰不會呢？

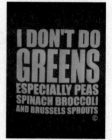

SNUGLO 的圖案設計

* · 妳最喜歡的牌子或人物（可以是任何領域的）以及理由？
  執掌 Gucci 和 YSL 的 Tom Ford（清楚強烈的視覺及美感）及 Miss Kitty（強勢的品牌，很酷的圖樣）。

* · 如果沒做這行妳會做什麼？
  要嘛做個全職媽咪，要不就美容師。

* · 妳還會想要挑戰哪一種行業呢？
  我想要試試女裝市場。

* · 妳的一天都怎麼度過的？
  設計、寄出訂貨、跟供應商訂材料、稅務處理、回覆電郵及解答疑問等全混在一塊兒，還有照顧我兩個女兒。

* · 對妳來說，全世界最能激發妳靈感的事物是什麼？
  我的孩子。

* · 一星期中妳最喜愛哪一天？理由為何？
  星期五，我的休假日，可以陪小孩。

* · 一星期中妳最討厭哪一天？理由為何？
  參考上題──開玩笑的啦！

* · 妳通常如何打發時間？
  我沒時間可以打發。

* · 妳的聖典為何？
  Vogue 雜誌。

* · 妳此刻讀些什麼書？書的內容是什麼？
  Boo Hoo，是關於 www.boo.com 這個網站的倒閉，這是網路事業崩盤時的第一樁大型意外事件。

Your favourite brand or character (can be in any category) and the reason?
Tom Ford for Gucci + YSL (clear strong vision and aesthetic), Miss Kitty (strong brand, cool graphics).

What would you be doing if you weren't designing?
I'd either be a full time mum or beautician.

What other forms of business would you like to venture into one day?
I would like to explore the womenswear market.

What is a typical day like for you?
A real mixture of designing, sending out orders, ordering from suppliers, vat returns, answering e-mails / inquiries etc and looking after my two little girls.

What is the most inspiring thing in the world for you?
My children.

What is your favourite day of the week? And why?
Friday. My day off work with my children.

What is your least favourite day of the week? And why?
See above. Only joking!

What do you do to kill time?
I have no time to kill.

What's your bible?
Vogue.

What book are you reading at the moment? And what's it about?
'Boo hoo' about the demise of the website www.boo.com the first big casualty in the .com crash.

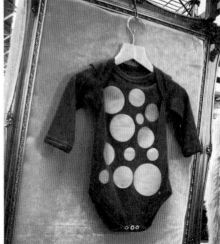

snuglo

www.snuglo.com
made in england

100% luxu
machine wa
made in en

www. snuglo

SNUGLO 小衣服的完整包裝

✽ · 妳最喜愛和最討厭倫敦哪一點？

我喜歡它的多元化，可以自由地去做很多事情，還有，沒有人認識你。我討厭它的污染、交通和高昂的物價。

✽ · 當工作或思考遇到瓶頸時，妳都怎麼做？

繼續克服它，如果真的無法克服我會先將它擱著，一會兒再回來看看，如果仍然行不通我就不做了。

✽ · 妳如何應付妳的壓力？

看電視和跑步。

✽ · 妳現在過的是妳夢想中的生活嗎？如果不是，妳夢想中的生活型態及地點為何？

是的，但希望能有更多休閒時間好讓我去旅行。

✽ · 讓妳維持生活步調及常規的事物是什麼？

想法，以及這個世界持續給予我的靈感。

✽ · 妳最喜歡的飲料、音樂類型和電影各是什麼？

可樂和香檳（分開來喝）；所有類型的音樂；《BJ 單身日記》。

✽ · 怎麼樣會特別討妳開心？

跟我老公出去吃頓晚餐。

✽ · 妳通常都怎麼烹調馬鈴薯？

水煮或烘烤。

✽ · 夢想中的工作是？

做我自己公司的設計總監，擁有完全的藝術品質控制權，但由他人來經營公司。

✽ · 什麼是妳從沒有嘗試過、但有一天一定會去做的一件事？

學開車。

✽ · 最近迷些什麼事物？

我的兩個女兒。

✽ · 什麼是妳生活中不可或缺的？

我的家庭。

✽ · 請用簡單的一句話來形容妳自己。

很沒有組織、藝術家性格、浪漫、仁慈、滑稽又令人驚奇。

✽ · 要不要跟大家分享妳的祕密？

活在當下。

✽ · 夢想能……

成為任何你想要成為的人事物。

What do you love and hate the most about London?
I love the diversity, there's lots of things to do, the annominity. I hate the pollution, traffic and expensive.

What do you do when you are stuck on a particular design/idea?
Keep going over it, if I'm really stuck I leave it to one side and come back to it, if it's still not working I won't do it.

How do you handle your stress?
Watching TV and running.

Are you living your ideal lifestyle right now? If not, what's your ideal lifestyle & place to be?
Yes, but I'd like more time off to travel.

What keeps you going and stay in tune?
Ideas and constant inspiration from the world around me.

What's your favourite drink, music & film?
Coke and champagne (separately). All types of music. *Bridget Jones.*

What would be a special treat for you?
Going out for dinner with my husband.

What's your usual way of cooking potato?
Boiled or baked.

A dream job to you is...
Being a design director for my own company, with complete artistic control, but having other people managing it.

What have you not tried to do, but would definitely want to try one day?
Learn to drive.

What is your latest obsession?
My two daughters.

What can't you live without?
My family.

Please describe yourself in a short sentence.
Unorganised, artistic, romantic, kind, funny and fabulous.

Dare to share one of your secrets?
Live in the moment.

Dream to be...
Anything you want to be.

可愛的嬰兒帽子

ПЄTTY & МАTTY

Annette Kimmings & Matthew Sheldon

www.nettyandmatty.com
info@nettyandmatty.com
sell at 'Our Shop' & nettyandmatty.com (via e-mail)
shop address: 2.8 Kingly Court, Carnaby Street, London W1B 5PW
(info@thisisourshop.co.uk)
+44 (0) 20 7434 2141

左：Annette；右：Mattew 和他們創作的娃娃

中間這一排照片為 Annette 將自己裝扮成娃娃的照片

這些穿著蓬蓬蕾絲花邊裙的女娃娃，檸檬黃、霓虹、土耳其藍、湖水綠，打扮有如調色盤般的繽紛，像極了剛從 fashion 秀中走出來的模特兒。她們都有著漫畫風格大大的眼睛和紅紅的臉頰，俏皮可愛，但卻也隱隱透露出許古怪以及瘋狂的元素。"Hey!" 她們說：「歡迎來到 NETTY & MATTY 的世界！」NETTY & MATTY 的作品主要就是將這些俏麗女娃娃的照片，印刷在背包上；每個包包都有不同的情境小故事，呈現出變調有趣的天真；加上誇張色彩的運用，讓這些包包看起來玩味十足。

整個 NETTY & MATTY 的概念是由 Annette 跨越在真人與童話邊緣的世界中延伸出來的。大學期間學的是服裝織品系，Annette 的作品頻頻反應出她對玩偶和卡通的狂熱，設計主題往往離不開虛擬的童話世界。此外，她更不時將自己化身塑造為布偶或玩具來表現想法，放肆的創意充滿戲劇效果。大學時期就開始交往的男友 Matthew，學的則是純藝術。但他的重心似乎都放在搞樂團和女友身上，經常為了幫 Annette 拍照或參與她的作業製作而忽略了自己的課業，不過兩人也因此培養出合作的默契。去年大學畢業之後，兩個人決定以 Annette 創造的這些女娃娃作為產品主角，以他們名字的簡稱為名成立了 NETTY & MATTY 品牌。

畢業的這一年來，Annette 和 Matthew 在平常工作之餘，參加小型設計展、市集，嘗試到不同店家去推銷 NETTY & MATTY。整個過程中他們面臨到自創品牌的資金不足和製造的困難，可是因為做的是自己內心真正喜歡的事，所以他們一步一步穩穩的走，沒有夢想一飛沖天的不切實際，也沒有放棄而停下腳步。對 Annette 而言，娃娃就是生命，她對娃娃瘋狂的程度可以用重量級來形容，她甚至表示她的希望是擁有一個長得跟 Hello Kitty 一模一樣的小孩！

回想起自己創造品牌所累積的挫折和經驗，讓我在面對這些剛踏出校門不久的社會新鮮人經營自創品牌的艱辛過程時都加倍感同深受。成立品牌很容易，如何經營塑造它才是真正長跑的開始。我很喜歡 Annette 和 Matthew 新鮮的點子和搶眼的作品，也希望能在未來看到更多 NETTY & MATTY 的娃娃搖擺起舞在不同的產品上！

Annette 的手繪本

＊‧跟我們談談 NETTY & MATTY 及你們的背景。你們是如何想出這個名稱及整個概念的？

Matthew 我是 Matt，我跟 Annette 是工作夥伴，在 Milton Keynes 生活及工作。我們在技術學院認識並且偶然地上了同一所大學。在那裡，Annette 學的是時裝及織品，而我主修純藝術。大學期間我們總是互相幫忙，給予對方作品意見。她大三時我幫她處理影像及 CAD 作業部份，好讓她能有更多時間專注在更重要的事物上。到她畢業時，繼續合作似乎就成了最自然的事。這個牌子的概念來自 Annette，主要跟她貫穿整個大學時代的想法和她對舊玩具和洋娃娃的喜愛有關，但是透過影像和拼貼呈現出來的則是我們倆合作的成果。NETTY & MATTY 這個名字是我想出來的，我平常暱稱 Annette 'Netty'，後來朋友們也跟著這麼叫，有時候大家叫我 Matty──這也許是因為大家叫她 Netty，所以也要這樣叫我的原因。Netty & Matty，這兩個名字放在一起似乎配得挺好的，後面都有個 tty，而且視覺上看起來也很對稱。我們那時必須趕快決定名稱好讓架站事務進行，Annette 本來不喜歡這個名字，不過也想不出別的更好的──雖然她現在對這個名字很滿意。

＊‧透過 NETTY & MATTY，你們想跟大家表達些什麼呢？

表達我們自己。我們都是非常視覺系的人，所以設計一些視覺感官的東西是很自然的事，雖然我們也希望這些作品能同時表達出一種新奇感。我們同時灌注了很多關懷、專注及愛在裡頭，也很希望這些訊息能透過作品傳達出來。

＊‧你們的產品有哪些種類？還想觸及哪些領域？

我們設計並且製作袋子，目前有三種類型：棉質包包（二十五種不同設計）、皮質小背包（四種設計，我們會擴展此項產品，因為它們跟棉質包包有很類似的視覺設計）及娃娃包（因為是委託製造性質，所以我們保證每一個都是獨一無二的）。我們終會擴大產品領域，也許甚至超出時尚範圍，因為我覺得，「視覺」是整個概念和表現的基礎，它比表達的形式為何要來得重要，例如袋子。同樣的例子，看板是廣告的最佳媒介，雜誌可以記載許多資訊，袋子對我們來說是一個相當方便的形式，但我們並不會把自己侷限在這裡。我們曾談過也許有一天會往服裝品牌發展，也希望有一天能創作兒童繪本。

Tell us a bit about NETTY & MATTY and your background. How did you come up with the name and concept?

Matthew I'm Matt and I work with Annette. We live and work in Milton Keynes. We met at college and then by chance went to the same university. Annette did a fashion and textiles degree and I did a fine art degree. Throughout our time at university we were always helping each other out, chipping in ideas for each others work. During Annette's 3rd year I helped her out with photo and CAD work so that she could concentrate on the more important stuff. After she finished it just seemed logical to carry on working together. The initial concept was Annette's idea as it came through her university work and her love of old toys and dolls, but through the photos and collages we did it evolved and developed between us both. I thought of the name.

I started to call Annette 'netty' and it caught on with friends, and sometimes I was called 'matty', probably as a reference to people calling Annette 'netty'.

The name NETTY & MATTY just seemed to fit nicely with both names having the tty bit and visually they went well together. We had to decide on the name so as to get a web-site going, Annette wasn't keen on it at first but because she couldn't think of anything better we went with it, although she's happy with it now!

What are you expressing through NETTY & MATTY?

We are expressing ourselves. We are both very visual people and it just seems natural to continue producing visuals, although we would like to think that the work also expresses a sense of fun. There is a lot of care, attention and love that goes into it, and we would hope that would come through also.

What product range do you have? And what to expand?

We design and make bags, we have three different types at the moment, cotton bags (25 different designs), leather satchels (4 designs, although this will expand as they use similar imagery to the cotton bags) and dolly bags. (which are made on a commission basis, which makes each doll a one off.) We will expand our range eventually, maybe even out of the realm of fashion, as I think that the imagery is where the idea and expression lies, and that's more important than the form it is expressed in, i.e. the bag. In the same way that the billboard is a carrier of the advert, or the magazine is a vehicle for the information within, the bags are a convenient form for us, and I don't think we will limit ourselves to them indefinitely. We have spoken about maybe do a clothing collection one day. We would also love to write and illustrate a children's book.

Please describe your working procedure.

Matthew We usually start by talking about what we want to do and how we can go about it. Then either one of us will make something (like Annette making the dolls) or we will gather some images together, mostly photos, or I will put stuff together on the computer. Throughout though we are always talking to each other asking opinions etc. When we are happy with what we have we then have to decide what form would best suit the ideas and images. We do not think of ourselves as exclusively bag designers, we just felt that what we are currently doing worked well in the form it took. After all of this we go into production and Annette will mostly do most of the machine work, and I help out where I can, usually with the finishing touches. (as most of my work is done!)

＊．請談談你們工作的程序。

通常我們會先談談想要做些什麼以及如何著手進行。然後嘛我們其中一人會去做一些東西（例如Annette 會做娃娃）或是把一些影像收集起來一大部份是照片，或者我會把收集來的資料全部放進電腦編排。整個過程我們都會不斷地詢問對方的意見，等我們都滿意了，才會開始去想到底要以何種形式來表現這些影像，我們並不完全自視為「提袋設計師」，只是覺得目前為止我們所要表達的東西透過袋子來表現還蠻不錯的。在這之後我們會進入製作階段，Annette 負責大部份的機械作業，我則視情況幫忙（既然我大部份的任務已經結束了！），通常是完成作業最後一部份的細節的檢視。

Netty & Matty 的包包

＊‧ 你們如何宣傳並販賣你們的產品？

大部份是透過網站，雖然我們也透過倫敦 Carnaby St. 上一間很酷的小店來賣。我們才剛起步，還在學習怎麼作業，所以希望能把產品擴展到一些賣場，雖然那也得視我們製作的產品而定。

＊‧ 你們對 NETTY & MATTY 的想法及欲達成目標為何？

要有創造力、能做我們想做的事，以及最重要的——要能從中得到樂趣！

＊‧ 從你們開始這個品牌作業以來，讓你感到最開心的事情是什麼？最難過的呢？

我想對我們倆來說最美妙的時刻莫過於另類時尚週，在有人看到我們的作品後臉上露出笑容的那一刻！看見那麼多人對我們的作品表現出快樂甚或喜悅的表情真是非常非常棒的一件事！在發展的現階段其實大部分的事物都很困難。我想我們不是唯一身在其中的，任何一位想要起步的創意工作者都會感到如此。艱難的時刻總是讓人傷心，我保證每年都有成千上萬的好創意因為實行上有困難而被迫放棄。唯一真能幫得上忙的（就我們所知）是 The Prince's Trust，但也不好申請，而且他們也不是完全那麼幫得上忙——至少就我們的經驗來說是吧。

＊‧ 你們是怎麼開始注意時尚及配件這個行業，並進而產生興趣？

我們發現我們所觸及的範圍或多或少都跟流行沾上邊，然而即使如此，我們也並不完全對它感興趣。我想我們跟其他任何人一樣在成長過程中注意到時尚及配件這些玩意，但很顯然地，身為一個女孩，Annette 比我注意得更多！像我之前所說的，時尚及配件對我而言只是非常方便的一個媒介。但我們不想對時尚界抱著輕率的態度，因為它是個很有趣的領域，而且也相當適合現階段我們所做的東西，而且可以看到它的後續發展。比起大聲疾呼「我們是提袋設計師，永遠都會是」，我們更享受被自己的想法帶著走的感覺。

＊‧ 你們有任何其它工作嗎？

Annette 我在本地一所幼稚園當美術老師，教三到七歲小朋友。

Matthew 我最近開始了自由攝影師及設計師的工作。

How do you promote and sell your products?

Through our web-site mainly, although we also sell through a cool little shop just off Carnaby St. in London. It's still early days and we are learning how to do things, so we hope to expand to other outlets in the near future, although this is dependant on what we are producing.

What's your vision and mission for NETTY & MATTY?

To be creative, be able to do what we want, and most of all, to have fun!

Since you started your brand, what has been the most joyful thing that has happened to you? And the most difficult?

I think the best moments for us both were at alternative fashion week, whenever we saw someone looking at our stuff smiling! Just seeing so many people have a happy even joyful reaction to what we do was very very nice! At this stage in our development most things are pretty difficult. I don't think we are alone in this, anyone leaving a creative degree who wants to start something has a hard time. I think it's a sad thing that it's so hard, I'm positive that tons of genuine talent is wasted each year because of the difficulty. The only real help (that we know of anyway) is the Prince's Trust, and even that's pretty hard to get through, and they aren't always that helpful, at least from our experience anyway.

How did you first become aware of and become interested in fashion & accessories?

We are aware that to a certain extent we are involved in 'fashion' and even if what we do falls within its boundaries we aren't really interested in 'fashion'. I suppose we became aware of fashion & accessories at the same time as anyone else does, while growing up, but obviously Annette being a girl was more aware than I was! Like I said before 'fashion and accessories' is just a convenient vehicle for what we do at the moment. We are not trying to be flippant about fashion as it is a very interesting place, and it fits what we are currently doing very well, which we can see continuing. We just enjoy letting ideas take us where they will, rather than saying, 'we are bag designers, and forever will be'.

Do you have any other job?

Annette I work as an art teacher in a local Prep school, teaching 3-7 year olds.

Matthew I have recently started working as a freelance photographer/designer.

朋友在 Party 時抱著 Netty & Matty 娃娃

✲‧ 跟彼此一起工作有什麼感覺？（最開心和最痛苦的時候）

Annette 跟 Matt 共事很有趣。和腦波波長相同的人一起工作是很棒的事，即使我們倆是那麼地不同。沒有什麼痛苦的事發生啦。

Matthew 我喜歡跟 Netty 一起工作，她非常有創造力，而且總是活力充沛。和一個你深深信任的人一起腦力激盪是相當棒的。最痛苦的時刻莫過於我們該決定要用哪個圖案又無法下決定的時候（Netty 比較常這樣），因為我們總是設計出很多圖案，導致選取上非常困難。對我來說最快樂的時刻是我們一起坐下來設計或構思新的構圖時，通常那是非常令人興奮的！

✲‧ 你們的「必要配件」是什麼？

Annette 一頂超酷的帽子。

Matthew 沒有，任何被宣稱為「必要配件」的東西都是騙人的！

✲‧ 你們會從以前或當代的一些藝術家或設計師的作品尋找靈感嗎？

Annette 會，但主要是由插畫家那兒，而不是從服裝設計師那兒。我收集舊的兒童書籍並且間接地從它們那兒找到靈感。如果要列舉一個插畫家，我會說 Sara Fanelli 給了我很多啟發。

Matthew 如果是針對 NETTY & MATTY 這個點子，那我沒有直接從哪裡得到靈感，雖然我一直很相信萬物必定互相影響——即使只是無意識地。沒有任何事物是百分之百原創。

✲‧ 你們最喜歡的牌子或人物（可以是任何領域的）是什麼？理由為何？

Annette 我沒有最喜歡的牌子，但我挺喜歡 Eley Kishimoto 和 Antoni & Alison，因為他們的設計玩味十足，簡單卻又有飽合、實驗性強的印刷。

Matthew 也許是蘋果電腦吧！他們度過低潮期，一回到市場上就創造出最棒的產品——地球上最有設計感的電腦和配件！我也喜歡 Jeff Koons。我想，當一名藝術家把自己變成一個品牌時，他要不是個天才，就是個白痴。像是 Andy Warhol 這一類的人在現今就是如此被看待的。但 Koons 不同之處在於：他自己本身就是個品牌，不只是他的作品。

✲‧ 如果不是做這行，你們會做些什麼呢？

Annette 睡覺、東整理西整理，或吃東西。

Matthew 做別行。

✲‧ 你們還會想要挑戰哪一種行業？

Annette 我想挑戰兒童繪本文集。

Matthew 跟 Annette 一樣出一本書，另外我覺得再回去玩樂團好像也不錯。（不過我不確定那算不算一種「行業」？）

✲‧ 描述你們的一天吧！

Annette 又累、又吵、又亂。

Matthew 無聊的、有趣的、累人的。

✲‧ 世界上最能激發你們靈感的東西？

Annette 看到有創造力的人。我喜歡看到有創造力的人，而因為我的工作是教小朋友畫畫所以我總是可以看到這些，那很特別。現今社會應該多強調創造力的重要性。

Matthew 沒有特定的事物，雖然我的確發現讓自己置身於富創造力的環境中可以激發我的靈感：去看展覽、看電影或聽我真的很喜歡的音樂。甚至只是去讀關於它們的東西（例如讀一本藝術相關的書籍等）。

✲‧ 一星期中你們最喜愛的一天？理由為何？

Annette 星期天，我也不確定我是怎麼發現它是一星期中最能讓人放鬆的一天的。

Matthew 星期六和星期日，因為可以跟 Netty 多一點時間相處。

✲‧ 一星期中你們最討厭的一天呢？理由呢？

Annette 沒有。

Matthew 沒有。

✲‧ 平日你們如何打發時間？

Annette 做我自己的玩具和衣服。

Matthew 聽音樂、玩電腦遊戲、閱讀、看電視電影、上網亂逛。

What is it like to work with each other? (the happiest and most painful moments)

Annette Working with Matt is Fun. It's nice to work with someone that's on the same wavelength, even though we are quite different! Nothing stands out as being painful.

Matthew I love working with Netty, she's so creative and has so much energy. It's great to have someone you trust so deeply to bounce ideas between. The most painful moments are usually when we have to decide on an image, and we are quite indecisive (Netty more so!) as we usually create so many visuals that it's very hard to come to a decision. The best moments for me are when we are sitting down together designing or coming up with new visuals, it's usually a quite exiting time!

What is a 'must-have' accessory to you?

Annette A good poncy hat!

Matthew Nothing. Anything that claims to be a 'must have' is lying!

Do you draw inspiration from the work of other designers - historic or contemporary?

Annette Yes but not fashion designers, mainly illustrators. I collect old children's books, and indirectly draw a lot of inspiration from them. To name an illustrator I would say that Sara Fanelli is a big inspiration.

Matthew In reference to Netty & Matty then no not directly, although I am a believer in the fact that everything influences everything else, even if it's subconscious. Nothing is 100% original.

＊ 你們的「聖典」？

Annette 我沒有，不過二手店是我膜拜的地方。

Matthew 沒有，我不會把自己的信仰放在任何事物上。

＊ 你們最近讀些什麼書？書的內容是什麼？

Annette *The New Faber Book of Children's Verse*，有許多新舊童詩。

Matthew Mark Sturdy 所著的 *Pulp: Truth and Beauty*，是關於流行音樂團體 Pulp 的故事點滴。

Your favourite brand or character (can be in any category) and the reason?

Annette I don't have a favourite but I do like Eley Kishimoto and Antoni & Alison, because they are quirky with simple designs but bold and experimental print work.

Matthew Probably Apple. They came back from the brink to create the best working, most stylish computers and accessories on the planet! Also I like Jeff Koons. I think the fact that an artist turned himself into a 'brand' is either genius or utter stupidity! I think people like Warhol are looked at in the same way today, but with Koons I think it was on purpose, as he himself was the brand not just the things he did.

What would you be doing if you weren't doing this?

Annette Sleeping, tidying or eating.

Matthew Something else.

What other forms of business would you like to venture into one day?

Annette I would like to write and illustrate a children's book.

Matthew Like Annette I'd like to write and illustrate a book. Also to be in a band again would be cool. (not sure if that's a business though!)

What's a typical day like for you?

Annette Hectic, noisy and messy.

Matthew Boring, interesting, tiring.

What is the most inspiring thing in the world for you?

Annette Seeing people being creative. I like seeing people being creative, and because I work in a school I see children doing it all the time, and it's a special thing. There should be more emphasis on creativity in today's society.

Matthew Nothing in particular, although I do find involving myself in creative things inspires me, whether that's going to an exhibition, watching a good movie, hearing music I really like. Or even just reading about them. (like reading an art book etc...)

What is your favourite day of the week? And why?

Annette Sunday, not sure why I just find it the most relaxing day of the week.

Matthew Saturday and Sunday, because I get to spend more time with Netty.

What is your least favourite day of the week? And why?

Annette I don't have one.

Matthew I don't have one.

What do you do to kill time?

Annette I make toys and clothes for myself.

Matthew Listen to music, play computer games, read a book, watch a movie/TV, surf the net.

What's your bible?

Annette I don't have one but second-hand shops are my place of worship!

Matthew Nothing, I wouldn't put my faith in any one thing.

What book are you reading at the moment? And what's it about?

Annette *The New Faber Book of Children's Verse*. It's full of old and new children's poems.

Matthew '"Pulp" - Truth and Beauty' by Mark Sturdy. It's about the pop group Pulp.

Annette 裝扮成娃娃的照片

＊‧ 你們最喜歡和最討厭倫敦的哪一點？
Annette 我喜歡這城市的各種可能性，討厭具侵略性的、憤世嫉俗的和無禮的人。
Matthew 我喜歡的一點是你可以在這裡找到任何你想吃的食物類型，我喜歡這裡有好的唱片行和書店，我喜歡倫敦給你的任何未知數。我討厭在倫敦開車，我討厭人群。

＊‧ 當設計或思考遇到瓶頸時你們都怎麼做？
Annette 跟 Matt 聊聊。
Matthew 休息一下，如果 Netty 在就跟她聊，問問她的意見。

＊‧ 你們如何應付壓力？
Annette 泡個澡。
Matthew 我應付得很好！

＊‧ 你們現在過的是夢想中的生活嗎？如果不是，你們夢想中的生活型態及地點為何？
Annette 不，我現在仍住家裡。夢想中的生活是能跟 Matt 住在一起。
Matthew （請參考 Annette 的答案！）

＊‧ 讓你們維持生活步調及常規的事物是什麼？
Annette 音樂、到倫敦去、觀察人群。
Matthew Annette。

＊‧ 你們最喜愛的飲料、音樂類型及電影為何？
Annette 鳳梨椰奶霜（Pina Colada，雞尾酒名）、硬地音樂（Indie，完全獨立製作的音樂）/ 另類音樂、《艾蜜莉的異想世界》。
Matthew 可樂。太多了，任何與眾不同或有趣的音樂和電影我都愛。

＊‧ 怎麼樣會特別討你們開心？
Annette 吃壽司。
Matthew 去吃頓好的或晚上出去找樂子。（在 Milton Keynes 這個地區，要辦到這些非常不容易——當你在各方面是如此與眾不同時！）

＊‧ 你們平時怎麼烹調馬鈴薯？
Annette 烤，加很多奶油、起司和美乃滋！
Matthew 馬鈴薯煎餅，先磨、攪拌然後煎煮。

＊‧ 夢想中的工作是？
Annette 開心、又有創造力地去做我喜歡的事。
Matthew 做我喜歡做的事。

What do you love and hate the most about London?
Annette   I love the possibilities, I dislike aggressive/angry/rude people.
Matthew   I love that you can get any type of food you want, I love that there are good record and book shops, I love the anonymity London give you. I hate driving in London, I hate the crowds.

What do you do when you are stuck on a particular design/idea?
Annette Talk to Matt.
Matthew   Take a break, and if Netty's about talk to her, ask her opinion.

How do you handle your stress?
Annette Take a bath.
Matthew   Pretty well!

Are you living your ideal lifestyle right now? If not, what's your ideal lifestyle & place to be?
Annette No, now I am still living at home, ideally I just want to live with Matt.
Matthew   (see Annette's answer!)

What keeps you going and stay in tune?
Annette   Music, going to London, people watching.
Matthew   Annette.

What's your favourite drink, music & film?
Annette   Pina Colada, indie/alternative, Amelie.
Matthew   Coke, too much to list, anything that does something different and interesting.

What would be a special treat for you?
Annette   Sushi.
Matthew   Going for a nice meal or having a fun night out. (which in Milton Keynes is pretty tough if your in any way different!)

What's your usual way of cooking potato?
Annette Baking, with lots of butter, cheese and mayo!
Matthew   Potato pancakes, grate, make and then fry.

A dream job to you is...
Annette   Being happy and creative while doing something I enjoy.
Matthew   Something I enjoy.

What have you not tried to do, but would definitely want to try one day?
Annette   Write a children's book, and live in New York.
Matthew   To travel.

What is your latest obsession?
Annette   Taking photos. (mainly of myself!)
Matthew   Netty & Matty.

What can't you live without?
Annette   Matt.
Matthew   Annette.
(this was not premeditated!)

Please describe yourself in a short sentence.
Annette Shy, scatty, poser, big eyes, creative.
Matthew   I am a lazy, (ish) tidy, perfectionist.

Dare to share one of your secrets?
Annette   I am a compulsive tidier. (even though I'm very messy.)
Matthew   Secrets, I have none!

Dream to be...
Annette   ...A dreamer.
Matthew   ...Happy.

＊．什麼是你們從沒嘗試過、但哪一天一定會去做的事？
Annette 寫本童書，定居紐約。
Matthew 旅行。

＊．最近迷些什麼？
Annette 拍照（大多是自拍！）
Matthew NETTY & MATTY。

＊．什麼是你們生活中不能缺少的？
Annette Matt。
Matthew Annette。
（我們沒有事先約好這樣回答哦！）

＊．請用簡短的句子描述你們自己。
Annette 害羞、瘋狂、愛裝腔作勢、大眼、有創造力。
Matthew 我是個懶惰的、蠻整齊的完美主義者。

＊．要不要跟大家分享你們的秘密？
Annette 我有潔癖（雖然我總是亂七八糟）。
Matthew 秘密，我沒有耶！

＊．夢想成為……
Annette 一個夢想家！
Matthew 快樂！

Leona Baker

www.ladyluckrulesok.com
leona@ladyluckrulesok.com
sell online and through 45 independent boutiques and galleries
around the world. Stockists are Our Shop in London, No Angel in
Manchester, Beams in Japan, Takeout in Australia, Las Vegas in
Sweden, Retro in Dublin and Missbehave in New York.

Leona 站在她辦公室的展示桌前

MATAZ

Ian
Dury

I'M A
MINI MINX

DO IT

Leona 收集的古董小飾品

個子小巧，長相甜美的 Leona 擁有一個首飾配件品牌 LADY LUCK RULES OK 以及經營成功的網路商店，我時常會在不同的雜誌上看見她的產品。她的首飾配件主要由不同的二手舊物、玩具和復古小東西組合而成。這類由舊物創造新潮的配件首飾在這兩三年開始放肆地流行起來，為了因應市場的需要，除了持續運用二手舊物之外，Leona 也漸漸開發新的配件來搭配她的設計。

走進 Leona 的工作室彷彿走進童年時期的夢想樂園，整個房間排滿了許多微笑的小鹿斑比和米老鼠，還有各式各樣的二手娃娃，和印有卡通圖案的舊瓶罐、鐵盒。展式桌上叮叮咚咚紅橙黃綠藍靛紫的首飾、鍊子、徽章，穿插擺設在這些早期的二手玩具及卡通產品之間，相映成趣。看到她的收藏成果，不禁讓我開始後悔沒有好好保存那些已被拋棄的童年玩物，如今卻必須花大把錢再去把這些舊物搜購回來的愚蠢行為。

Leona 從小就喜歡收集東西，開始是興趣，久了也變成一個習慣。任何讓她看得順眼、可愛有特色的東西她都會買下來收藏。逛 Charity Shop*、Car Boot Sale** 和跳蚤市場（現在又多了一個 eBay），找尋特別的二手舊物，一直是她最大的嗜好也是靈感來源。從她工作室和家裡的擺設就可以看出來，她很少採用新的傢具，連鏡子都是從 Charity Shop 扛回來、上面印有小鹿斑比圖案的舊鏡子。這些舊物在她大膽創新的搭配下，呈現出新商品找不到的韻味。

問她是如何開始自己的另類型首飾設計事業？她說離家之後來到倫敦，做了很多不同的工作。對 Fashion 的興趣來自於這幾年造型助理工作經驗的累積，因而開始在 Portobello Market 賣二手衣打零工賺錢。五年前，在無意間找到一批 80 年代的舊珠寶首飾，這些舊珠寶首飾的設計師啟發了 Leona 對這個領域的興趣，因為她從來沒有想過珠寶設計可以這麼多元、隨性、充滿創意。她開始將自己多年的小收藏品隨意搭配做成首飾配件來賣，之後，每個星期天她在市集

的攤位都被橫掃一空，受歡迎的程度連她自己都不敢相信！隨之而來的是許多雜誌的報導，採用她的產品去拍照作造型的媒體也不在少數。

Leona 表示有時候她真的不知道這一切是怎麼發生的，事業好像在不知不覺中自己成型。現在銷售穩定的網路商店和固定店家的訂單讓她不必再到市集擺攤，但尋找特別的二手舊物仍是她的最愛。事業剛起步的頭幾年，Leona 會跑跑英國各地的 Charity Shop 和 Car Boot Sale；現在有能力了，時常還可以飛到別的國家的跳蚤市場去挖寶。她開心的說：「我一直認為自己是一個收藏者，把收集來的東西設計、加工成產品來賣。興趣變成事業是始料未及的驚喜，因為我在工作的時候只覺得是在滿足自己的興趣。」

記得武伯伯***曾告訴我們：「人生中最重要的一件事就是培養興趣，至少要培養一個會讓你專注、用心去做的興趣。」我常常想起武伯伯的話，也覺得自己何等幸福，不但興趣與目前的工作息息相關，而且從中又培養了更多不同的興趣。碰到 Leona 之後，讓我更加堅信，有一個會讓你執迷的興趣在人生中扮演的地位是何等重要！

* Charity Shop：在英國到處都可以看到這些賣二手物品的店，他們收集二手衣物，再將收入所得捐給慈善機構。

** Car Boot Sale：通常在春、夏季的每個星期天早晨，把家中的二手貨、舊物放在車上載去賣，車子就是你的攤位；英國到處都有 Car Boot Sale 的地點，通常是在大草坪、學校操場、教堂廣場或停車場，大一點的 Car Boot Sale 可容納上百部車，運氣好的時候可以買到別人家的珍貴古董或收藏。

*** 武伯伯是我青梅竹馬好友的父親，飽讀詩書，通情達禮，是一位我非常敬愛的長者。

Leona 的二手舊物收藏

＊．跟我們談談 LADY LUCK RULES OK 這個牌子，妳是怎麼想到這個名稱及整體產品概念的？

這算是個快樂的意外吧！以前我在 Portobello Market 有個攤位，販賣我從車庫拍賣買來的一些舊衣服，結果有一天我發現了一大堆 1980 年代的首飾，這些令人驚喜的飾品包括小型塑膠飛機、迷你電話機、開瓶器及含吸管的可樂大口杯，我從不知道首飾能這麼多樣好玩！後來我跟這些八〇年代首飾的設計者成了朋友，她激發了我成為一名飾品設計師的想法。後來我停止販賣舊衣服，開始專心改賣這些新鮮首飾玩意兒之後，每個星期六我的攤位都被客人洗劫一空，非常受歡迎。

＊．妳透過 LADY LUCK RULES OK 想跟大家表達些什麼呢？

趣味！趣味！趣味！我希望我的顧客們在穿戴這些飾品時，能像我當初發現然後製造它們的時候一樣開心。

＊．妳是如何把這個品牌打入市場的？

從第一次發現那些庫存首飾的當下，我就決定為它們創造一個品牌，好讓人們知道它們的來源。我設計了一個商標，取名為 LADY LUCK RULES OK——來自我幸運的首飾大發現之後。我印製了一些基本吊牌，還做了一箱徽章別針發送，當時有個朋友在紐約的 Nylon 雜誌實習，她為我的發現寫了一篇報導，之後就陸續有一些店家跟我聯絡（法國名店 Colette 曾 e-mail 給我，但沒有採購）。接著有更多報章雜誌寫了相關報導，包括 The Face、Sleazenation 及《衛報》(The Guardian) 等。

＊．請介紹一下妳自己並告訴大家妳的背景。

我是 Leona Baker，離鄉背井來到倫敦闖天下。在做了一連串怪異又好玩的工作後（時裝助理、女侍、鞋子採購員、市集販賣、櫥窗設計等），我定下心來，做自己的老闆。

Tell us a bit about LADY LUCK RULES OK. How did you come up with the name and concept.

It was all a happy accident - I had a stall at Portobello Market selling vintage clothing I'd sourced from car boot sales and one day I discovered a huge stash of 1980's dead stock jewellery. The exciting find included little plastic aeroplanes, mini telephones, neon bottle top openers, cola beakers with straws, I didn't know jewellery could be such fun! I became friends with the lady who had designed it all in the 80's and she inspired me to become a jewellery designer. I stopped selling clothing and piled my stall high with rainbow hued novelty trinkets and I was mobbed every Saturday.

What are you expressing through LADY LUCK RULES OK?

FUN ! FUN! FUN! I hope my customers have as much fun wearing the jewellery as I have sourcing and making it.

How did you launch the brand onto the market?

From the minute I had my first dead stock find I wanted to create a label so people knew where the pieces had come from. I designed a logo and christened the label LADY LUCK RULES OK - after my lucky dead stock find. I printed up some basic swing tags and made a tub of button badges to give away. My friend was in New York at the time doing work experience for *Nylon* and she wrote a news article about my find and from this I was contacted by stores wanting to sell my products (Colette e-mailed, but didn't buy) and more press wrote pieces including The *Face*, *Sleazenation* and *The Guardian*.

Please introduce yourself and tell us about your background.

My name is Leona Baker and I ran away from home to make my fortune in London. After a series of weird and wonderful jobs (fashion assistant, chamber maid, footwear buyer, market trader, window dresser) I have settled down to work for myself.

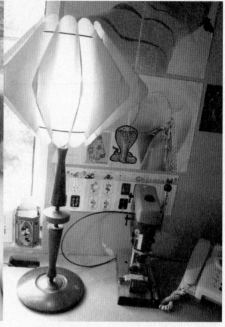

＊ · 妳是何時開始注意到時裝配件工業並進而對它產生興趣的？

一直都有。我媽媽在八〇年代是個非常時髦的女人，我常被她的大波浪捲髮和大型耳環搞得目眩神迷，她甚至會塗藍色的眼影！

＊ · 妳的產品有哪些種類？還想將觸角伸向何處？

目前有八大款式，而每星期我都會為每一款式增添一些新的樣式。我沉迷於尋找新的材質，差不多整天都在做首飾，晚上坐在電視機前時也不例外。為了表達對二手流行文化的喜好，近來我增加了不同圖案的 T 恤，也打算把這些設計印在手提袋上。

＊ · 請跟大家描述一下妳的工作程序。

早上收 e-mail（還穿著睡衣呢！）、做一些行政工作和郵務作業，然後在大約午餐時分到郵局寄出網路訂貨，接下來的時間就設計飾品。每一星期我會花一天的時間做公關，然後一個月做一次簿記和會計工作（打哈欠）。最好玩的莫過於到處旅行尋找新的素材，我們常常在英國各地的小村莊露營，逛當地的慈善義賣店。我也會招待自己到歐洲各地逛逛不定期舉辦的跳蚤市場，柏林是我的最愛。

﹡‧妳如何推銷妳的產品？

　行銷是非常重要的——妳可能有最可愛的商品，卻沒人知道妳在賣這些東西。我將主力放在青少年及街頭流行雜誌、假日報及一些手工製品網站等媒體的報導上——它們是免費的，而且可以很輕易地吸引我鎖定的消費群。

﹡‧從妳開始這個品牌作業以來，讓妳感到最開心的事情是什麼？最難過的呢？

　所有從滿意的顧客那兒寄來的 e-mail，那是很大的鼓勵，促使我創造出更多產品。

﹡‧妳身上的必備配件是什麼？

　我喜歡戴又大又漂亮的、掛滿各種幸運符、標誌和玩具的手環。我將它們當手環戴，有時則在兩端接緞帶當成項鍊來戴。

﹡‧設計師是很難掌握的一個工作嗎？身為一位設計師的感想如何？

　很幸運地我也是手工藝這個網路社群的一員，透過部落格及網頁連結，收到很多來自這些也是獨立製作的手工藝伙伴們的鼓勵及互動。

﹡‧妳會從其他設計師作品上找靈感嗎？

　我比較傾向從歌詞和舊的唱片封面上找靈感。我的男友有令人驚訝的唱片收藏，而我很喜歡在他放這些唱片時一邊做我的飾品。

廚房的櫃子

How did you first become aware of your interest in fashion and accessories?
Since forever. My Mum was a real stylish lady and in the eighties I was dazzled by her mental perms and huge earrings, she could even pull off blue eyeshadow!

What product range do you have? And what are you expanding to?
I currently have 8 collections and I add new styles to them on a weekly basis. I'm obsessed with finding new materials and I pretty much make jewellery all day and then all night in front of the telly. I have recently added a range of tees which are a homage to the art of second hand shopping and I will be printing the designs on tote bags too.

Please describe your working procedure.
I check my e-mails in the morning (still in my pyjamas) then I do admin and shipping tasks and take a trip to the post office to send website orders around lunch time. For the rest of the day I set to work on making all the goodies. I spend a morning a week on PR and a day a month on book keeping and accounting (yawn).
The super fun bits are travelling away to source materials and we often go camping in little villages around the UK to trawl the local charity shops. I also treat myself to the occasional European flea market, Berlin is my favourite.

How do you promote your products?
Marketing is super important, you could have the cutest products and no one even knows your selling them. I focus on obtaining editorial in teen and street magazines, weekend newspapers and crafty websites - it's free and a direct route to attracting my target audience.

Since you started your brand, what has been the most joyful thing that has happened to you?
All the lovely e-mails I receive from happy customers. It's a real confidence boost and drives me to create more stuff.

What are the 'must have' accessories for you?
I adore huge charm bracelets stuffed full of quirky charms, badges and toys. I wear mine as a bracelet or I tie ribbon on both ends and wear as a necklace.

Is being a designer a difficult job to handle? How are you feeling being alone?
Luckily, I'm also part of the crafting community and there is lots of support and interaction from fellow indie crafters through weblogs and links pages.

Do you draw inspiration from the work of other designers?
I tend to draw more inspiration from song lyrics and old album covers. My boyfriend has an incredible record collection and I enjoy making jewellery while he's playing his records.

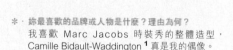

＊ · 一星期中妳最喜愛的一天？理由為何？
我喜歡星期天，因為不必擔心隔天得面對討厭的工作。

＊ · 妳都怎麼打發時間？
逛 eBay 網站找任何跟 Babycham 這個牌子有關的東西。

＊ · 妳最喜歡的品牌或人物是什麼？理由為何？
我喜歡 Marc Jacobs 時裝秀的整體造型，Camille Bidault-Waddington **1** 真是我的偶像。

＊ · 妳奉行不渝的寶典為何？
我收藏的那一大堆舊 *Nova* 雜誌。

＊ · 如果不是做這行，妳會從事什麼工作？
我會成為 Devo 樂團的第六名成員。

＊ · 妳最近讀些什麼書？書的內容是什麼？
赫曼·赫塞 (Herman Hesse) 的短篇小說集。其中一篇故事提到一位長笛演奏家，因為太迫切於想成為全世界最好的長笛演奏家，而失去了他的家人，孤獨以終老。

＊ · 妳還會想要挑戰哪一種行業？
我想在海邊經營一家便宜的 B&B 旅館（Bed & Breakfast，提供床鋪和早餐的家庭旅館）。裡頭有舊式的小型吧台和掛滿牆壁的木頭鴨子做裝飾。

＊ · 妳最喜愛和最討厭倫敦哪一點？
我喜歡坐在雙層巴士的上層，討厭人們的無禮。

＊ · 全世界最能激發妳靈感的事物？
讓父母以我為榮。

＊ · 當工作或思考遇到瓶頸時妳都怎麼做？
燒開水泡杯茶或咖啡。

1 歐洲知名造型師。

＊ · 妳如何應付壓力？
我會聽聽 Del Shannon 的 Runaway 這首歌。

What is your favourite brand or character and the reason?
I love the styling on the Marc Jacobs runway, Camille Bidault-Waddington is my hero.

What would you do if you weren't doing this?
I'd be the sixth member of Devo.

What other forms of business would you venture into one day?
I'd like to run a chintzy bed and breakfast by the sea side with a Delboy bar and flying ducks on the wall.

What is the most inspiring thing in the world to you?
Making my parents proud.

What is your favourite day of the week and why?
I like Sundays because I don't have to dread going to a job I hate the next day.

What do you do to kill time?
Trawl Ebay looking for anything Babycham related.

What's your bible?
My stack of vintage *Nova* magazines.

What book are you reading at the moment? And what's it about?
It's a book of short stories by Herman Hesse. One story is about a flute player who is so obsessed with being the best flute player in the world he looses his family and grows old alone.

What do you love and hate the most about london?
I love riding on the top deck of the old routemaster buses and hate the rudeness.

What do you do when you are stuck on a particular design/idea?
Put the kettle on.

How do you handle stress?
I listen to Runaway by Del Shannon.

* · 妳最喜歡的飲料、音樂類型和電影是什麼？
我喝一大堆自製的檸檬汁，常聽 Billy Childish 的歌，電影的話，我覺得勞勃 · 阿特曼 (Robert Altman) 1975 年執導的《納許維爾》(Nashville) 非常好看 (Shelley Duvall 飾演來自洛杉磯的 Joan 一角，她演得很棒)。

* · 怎麼樣能特別討妳開心？
在紐約的 CBGB（紐約著名的搖滾樂酒吧）看 Ramones 的演出（可惜這是不可能發生的事）。

* · 妳都怎麼烹調馬鈴薯？
做成馬鈴薯泥，配上法國酸奶油和青蔥。

* · 夢想中的工作是？
能穿著睡衣做飾品。

* · 最近迷些什麼？
用我新的徽章機器做徽章。

* · 什麼是妳生活中不可或缺的東西？
我的 i-pod 和 i-book，我是個蘋果電腦擁護者。

* · 請用簡單的一句話來形容妳自己。
一個不斷找尋樂趣、永遠無法下定決心的女孩。

* · 要不要跟大家分享妳的秘密？
我曾做過辣妹合唱團造型師的助理。

What's your favourite drink, music, film?
I guzzle pints of home made lemonade, I'm listening to
a lot of Billy Childish at the moment and the 1975 film
Nashville by Robert Altman is awesome. (Shelley Duvall
as LA Joan is a real treat.)

What would be a special treat for you?
To see the Ramones play at the CBGBs. (I'm sad this
can never happen.)

What's your usual way of cooking a potato?
Mashed with creme fraiche and spring onions.

A dream job to you is..
...making jewellery in my pyjamas.

What is your latest obsession?
Making button badges with my new badge machine.

What can't you live without?
My i-pod and i-book, I'm apple obsessed.

Please describe yourself in a short sentence.
A fun seeking girl who can never make her mind up.

Dare to share one of your secrets.
I used to assist the stylist that dressed the Spice Girls.

172

THE MAGNIFICENT CHATWIN BROTHERS

Sam Chatwin & Anselm Chatwin

www.themagnificentchatwinbros.co.uk
info@themagnificentchatwinbros.co.uk
sell at Beyond The Valley - 26 Ganton St, Soho, London
+44(0)7711 220 320 ; Labour of Love - 193 Upper Street, London
N11RQ +44 (0)20 7354 9333 ; Best - 5, Back Hill, London, EC1R
5EN, +44 (0)20 7833 5544 ; Saloon - 23 Arlington Way, London,
EC1 +44 (0)20 7278 4497 ; Into You - 144 St. John Street,
London EC1V 4AU, UK, +44 (020) 7253 5085 ;
www.holy-water.co.uk

左：弟弟 Anselm ；右：哥哥 Sam

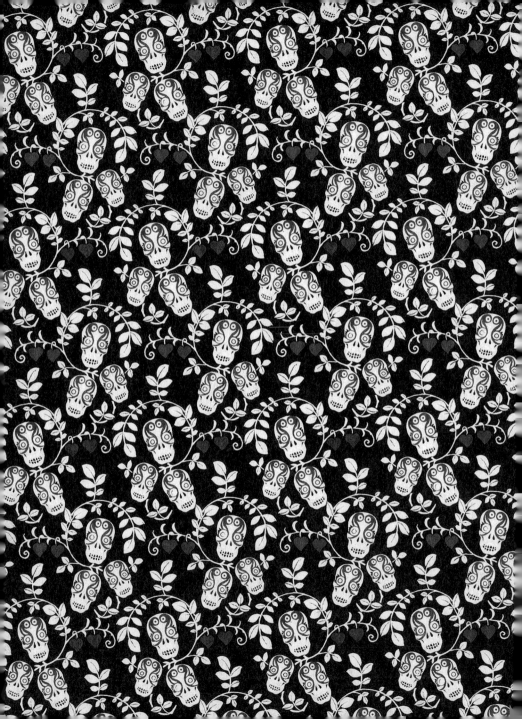

有次和 Tom* 閒聊時，他說起最近認識一對設計壁紙、包裝紙的兄弟，叫我一定要抽空去看看他們獨特的作品。我相信 Tom 的眼光，所以抽空去了他所說的那家店觀賞這對兄弟的作品。看了之後，果然沒有失望：古典混合新潮的搶眼圖像和顏色，純手工印刷，跳躍的霓虹、螢光黃、土耳其藍，不是父母們會選的那種壁紙，可是絕對是新一代壁紙和包裝紙中的川久保玲。剛開始我有點遲疑要不要訪問他們，因為他們並沒有在市集中設攤，跟我的主題不合。可是看過他們的作品和品牌名稱 THE MAGNIFICENT CHATWIN BROTHERS（完美無瑕的恰特溫兄弟）之後，我滿腦子好奇，怎麼能錯過認識這對「完美無瑕」的兄弟的機會呢？

第一次見到他們是在弟弟 Anselm 掌管的酒吧中，兩個人都高高瘦瘦的，外表不是很像。年齡相差五歲，哥哥 Sam 看起來比較性格，弟弟 Anselm 打扮時髦、比較含蓄。初次見面，當我還分不清誰是誰時，哥哥 Sam 開玩笑的說：「你只要記得我是比較有智慧的那個。」弟弟 Anselm 馬上不甘示弱的接著說：「我是長得比較好看的那個。」你一句我一句，喜歡同時講話亦或幫對方回話，兩個人在一起時調皮愛玩的情景，我想應該跟他們兒時沒什麼兩樣。正因為他們感情親密經常在一起，所以很多人都誤以為他們是 Gay Couple（同性戀人），久了他們也習以為常，有時還會以此為樂趣愚弄他人。

第二次正式訪問他們是在 Anselm 的家，新買不久，仍在裝潢中。他們各自有份正職工作，Sam 捨棄原本建築師的工作，現在是一家公關活動公司的首席

設計師；Anselm 年紀輕輕就掌管五家頗具名氣的酒吧，以 First Class** 的成績畢業於中央聖馬丁學院服裝設計系的他，擁有一個自創的獨立品牌 'Atomic Anselm'。

這對完美無瑕的兄弟出身藝術家庭（建築師爸爸，藝術家媽媽，作家姐姐，音樂家叔叔，還有很多，寫不完），他們兩個從小就展露過人的藝術天份，也都走上設計這條路。平常聊天之中總會提到一起做些設計來玩玩的想法，這個想法終於在 2004 年年底實踐——以他們彼此都很精通的平面和網版印刷設計做為起點，手印的壁紙和包裝紙產品才一上市就上了 *Timeout* 雜誌*** 、*Boom*！兄弟兩人對設計的看法默契十足，在活潑互動的情況之下盡情把玩創意，對他們而言，從這之中得到的樂趣比什麼都重要。

他們是我最後的一組訪問，訪問結束時已經晚上十點多了，大家都很餓（尤其以怕餓聞名的我能撐到十點實屬奇蹟！因為他們太有趣了！），所以我們一起到酒吧吃東西，同時慶祝我所有訪問的告一段落。在這裡我要謝謝完美無瑕的恰特溫兄弟為我的書做了一個完美無瑕的句點！

---

* Tom Shedden：出現在《創意市集》第一集中的攝影師。他最近搬家，幾乎所有時間都花在整修房子上。

** 英國大學績成績的區分方式：First Class、2-1、2-2、Third 和 Fail（當掉）。2005 年英國皇家威廉王子以 2-1 的成績光榮畢業，皇家成員都欣喜若狂（因為他是皇家子弟歷年來成績最好的一位）。First Class 是總成績中的最高榮譽，所以能以 First Class 的成績畢業實屬不易，也是無上光榮。

*** *Timeout* 雜誌：倫敦寶典，週刊。刊登每週倫敦的各種消息和活動，由靜到動，應有盡有。

Anselm 的素描

﹡ 請自我介紹，並談談 THE MAGNIFICENT CHATWIN BROTHERS 這個牌子背後的設計概念。

Sam 我是哥哥，THE MAGNIFICENT CHATWIN BROTHERS 這個雙人設計品牌的一員。概念是設計出我們自己都想擁有的漂亮手工藝品，融合傳統的英式設計，如 Charles FA Voysey 和他的「美術工藝運動」1，以及當代的視覺成像如刺青、爵士樂、漫畫等任何美國風的東西。比起量產，製造手工藝品總是樂趣無窮。

Anselm 我們是一對製造華麗手工藝品的兄弟。

﹡ 你們是何時決定一起工作？你們想透過作品傳達出什麼訊息呢？

Anselm 一直都想啊，然後有天就這麼決定了。

﹡ 你們有些什麼產品？還想延伸到什麼領域？

Sam 手工印製壁紙及包裝紙，還有手工鈕釦。想延伸到織布沙發及產品設計的領域。

Anselm 壁紙、包裝紙、鈕釦、版畫，及接下來的織物、燈具、磁磚等。

﹡ 你們如何宣傳並販賣你們的產品？

Sam 我們主要靠口耳相傳來達到宣傳效果。藉著倫敦的幾間店、網路及我們的網站來販賣產品。

Anselm 靠口耳相傳，至今效果似乎不壞。

---

1 美術工藝運動 (the Arts and Craft Movement)，十九世紀下半葉由於工業愈加發達導致設計水準下降，遂有人發起以傳統手工藝為主的運動，時間約從西元 1859 至 1910 年，Voysey 即為其中主要成員。

﹡ 從開始這個品牌以來，發生過最讓你們開心的事是什麼？最難過的呢？

Sam Time Out 雜誌對我們的設計做過的一整頁報導。

Anselm 最痛苦的是籌措資金，最開心的是被收錄在這本書裡。

﹡ 跟自己兄弟當同事的感覺如何（最開心和最痛苦的時候）？

Sam 很好，我很信任他的意見，而且合作愉快。我們各有所長，彼此互補得蠻好的。

Anselm 我們相處得超級好，所以相安無事，我可沒認識什麼可以和我爭辯粉紅色的正確投影色為何的人。

﹡ 你們對彼此的感覺如何？

Sam 他很棒。

Anselm 他超酷。

selm 的素描

Please introduce yourself and the concept behind THE MAGNIFICENT CHATWIN BROTHERS .
Sam   The older brother and one half of a London based design duo called the magnificent Chatwin Brothers. The concept being to design beautiful hand made objects that we would like to own ourselves, fusing traditional English design, such as Voysey and the Arts and Craft movement with contemporary imagery, including tattoos, Rockabilly, comics and Americana. Producing hand made rather than mass produced objects that always have a sense of fun.
Anselm   We are brothers who try to make magnificent products by hand.

When did you decide to work together?
Anselm   All ways talked about it and then one day it just happened.

What product range do you have? And what to expand?
Sam   Hand printed wallpaper and wrapping paper and hand made buttons. Expanding to fabric furniture and product design.
Anselm   Wallpaper, wrapping paper, buttons, art prints and soon fabrics, lights, tiles...

How do you promote and sell your products?
Sam   We self promote ourselves mainly through word of mouth. We sell our products in several shops in London, online and through our own website.
Anselm   Word of mouth seems to be working well so far.

Since you started the brand, what has been the most joyful thing that has happened to you? And the most difficult?
Sam   A full page spread in *Time Out* magazine on our designs.
Anselm   The most difficult is financing it all, and the best is being in this book.

What is it like to work with your brother? (the happiest and most painful moments)
Sam   Good. I trust his opinion and we work well together, our different skills complimenting each other well.
Anselm   We get on super well so it's pretty cool, I don't know many people I can argue about the exact shade of pink with.

What do you think of your brother?
Sam   He's great.
Anselm   He's super cool.

＊ · 你們有別的工作嗎？

Sam　有，在一間行銷活動公司擔任朝九晚五的首席設計師。

Anselm　有，一個領有執照的吧台經理人，並擁有自創 T 恤品牌。

＊ · 設計師是很難掌控的一個工作嗎？身為一位設計師的感覺如何？

Sam　不會，但跟其它工作一樣有好有壞。

Anselm　我太愛這個工作了，覺得能身為設計師是最幸運的一件事。

＊ · 你們會從以前或當代的一些藝術家或設計師作品找靈感嗎？

Sam　Alberto Vargas, Warhol, Saul Bass, Litchenstein, Sailor Jerry 等人，但我主要的靈感來自於從世界各地搜集來的一些東西。

Anselm　會的，所有我們看到的東西都會影響我們。特別是刺青、改造車、有關美國的文獻、搖滾樂、漫畫、卡通、爵士等。

＊ · 你們最喜歡的牌子或人物（可以是任何領域的）是什麼？理由為何？

Sam　丁丁，他真是無敵酷。

Anselm　丁丁，他是個痞子。

＊ · 你們還會想要挑戰哪一種行業呢？

Sam　想擁有自己的酒吧及比薩店。

Anselm　酒吧、藝廊、店面、傢俱設計。

＊ · 你們的一天通常是怎麼過的？

Anselm　起得太早、工作得太用力、玩樂太兒、太晚睡覺……

＊ · 全世界最能激發你們靈感的東西？

Sam　大自然，日常生活中的每樣事物。

＊ · 一星期中你們最喜愛的一天？理由為何？

Sam　星期六。

Anselm　星期天，可以跟我女友 Holly 約會。

＊ · 一星期中你們最討厭的一天呢？理由是？

Sam　星期一，朝九晚五的開始。

＊ · 平日你們如何打發時間？

Sam　睡覺、閱讀、看場電影、吃、喝、放屁、睡覺……

Anselm　我不大有時間供我打發。

＊ · 什麼是你們最信守不渝的聖典？

Anselm　*Time Out* 雜誌、*Icon* 雜誌。

Do you have any other job?

Sam　Yes, a 9 to 5 as head of design at an events company.

Anselm　Yes, manager/licensee of bars, own range of t-shirts.

Is being a designer a difficult job to handle? How are you feeling being one?

Sam　No, but has its good and bad days like any other job.

Anselm　Love it so much it really is the luckiest thing to be/do...

Do you draw inspiration from the work of other artists or designers - historic or contemporary?

Sam　Alberto Vargas, Warhol, Saul Bass, Litchenstein, Sailor Jerry to name a few but most of my inspiration comes from found objects from all over the world.

Anselm　Yes everything we see is an influence... Especially tattoos, hot rods, americana, rock and roll, comics, cartoons, rock-a-billy.

Your favourite brand or character (can be in any category) and the reason?

Sam　Tintin - he's fucking cool.

Anselm　Tintin - he's a dude.

What other forms of business would you like to venture into one day?

Sam　Would like to own my own bar and a pizza restaurant.

Anselm　Bars, art gallery, shop, furniture design.

What's a typical day like for you?

Anselm　get up too early, work too hard, party too hard, go to bed too late...

What is the most inspiring thing in the world for you?

Sam　Nature, everyday objects.

What is your favourite day of the week? And why?

Sam　Saturday.

Anselm　Sunday; get to hang out with Holly, my girlfriend.

What is your least favourite day of the week? And why?

Sam　Monday - start of the 9 to 5.

What do you do to kill time?

Sam　Sleep, read, go to the cinema, eat, drink, fart, sleep...

Anselm　I don't really have time to kill.

What's your bible?

Anselm　*Time Out, Icon.*

＊· 你們最近讀些什麼書？書的內容是什麼？

Sam　David Foster Wallace 的 *Girl with Curious Hair*。

Anselm　Sarah Hall 的 *The Electric Michaelangelo*，內容是描述一個男孩長大成人的過程，並如何學習成為一名刺青專家⋯⋯（目前唸到的部分）

＊· 你們最喜歡和最討厭倫敦的哪一點？

Sam　最討厭：地鐵、交通、牛津街、天氣、太多脾氣不好的人。還有，即便我在這裡出生長大，還是會迷路。最喜歡：還是地鐵、交通、牛津街、天氣、太多脾氣不好的人。還有，即便我在這裡出生長大，還是會迷路。

Anselm　我討厭設計不良的自行車專用道，喜歡這裡有太多可看可做的事。

＊· 當工作或思考遇到瓶頸時你們都怎麼做？

Sam　問我弟、放棄，並且說服自己從一開始這就是個愚蠢的想法、或是一直僵持直到思路通順為止。

Anselm　去做別的事再回來想。

＊· 你們如何應付壓力？

Sam　我處理得很糟！

Anselm　很糟，喝酒、抽煙、來回踱步⋯⋯

＊· 你們現在過的是夢想中的生活嗎？如果不是，你們夢想中的生活型態及地點為何？

Sam　希望能以 THE MAGNIFICENT CHATWIN BROTHERS 做為我的全職工作。

Anselm　我希望我是，有時你就是得不停鞭策自己⋯⋯

What book are you reading at the moment? And what's it about?

Sam   *Girl with Curious Hair* by David Foster Wallace.

Anselm   *The Electric Michelangelo* by Sarah Hall; it's about a boy growing up and learning to be a tatoo artist...(so far)

What do you love and hate the most about London?

Sam   Hate - The Tube, traffic, Oxford street, the weather, too many grumpy people, that I still can get lost in London after living here all my life.

Love   The Tube, traffic, Oxford street, the weather, too many grumpy people, that I still can get lost in London after living here all my life.

Anselm - I hate how bad the cycle lanes are. I love how much there is to see and do.

What do you do when you are stuck on a particular design/idea?

Sam   Ask my brother, give up and decide it was a stupid idea in the first place or stick with it until I work it out.

Anselm   Do something else and come back to it.

How do you handle your stress?

Sam   Badly.

Anselm   Badly; drink, smoke, pace...

Are you living your ideal lifestyle right now? If not, what's your ideal lifestyle & place to be?

Sam   Would love to be able to do THE MAGNIFICENT CHATWIN BROTHERS as a full time job.

Anselm   I hope I am, you just have to keep pushing all the time...

Anselm 小時候

Sam 小時候

Anselm 的自創品牌 Atomic Anselm

Chatwin Brothers 的壁紙 / 包裝紙圖騰

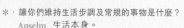

＊·讓你們維持生活步調及常規的事物是什麼？
Anselm　生活本身。

＊·你們最喜愛的飲料、音樂類型及電影為何？
Sam　健力士啤酒；鄉土搖滾 (Rockabilly)、鄉村、靈魂樂；電影為 *The Producers*、*Some Like It Hot* 及任何 Marx Brothers 的電影。
Anselm　Modello的啤酒、咖啡，The Cure 合唱團、The Pixies 樂團、ESG、The Supremes 三重唱、貓王。

＊·怎麼樣會特別討你們開心？
Anselm　讓我親眼看到貓王現場演唱會。

＊·你們平時怎麼烹調馬鈴薯？
Sam　用烤的。
Anselm　薯條。

＊·什麼是你們從沒嘗試過、但哪一天一定會去做的事？
Anselm　高空跳傘。

＊·最近迷些什麼？
Sam　霓虹粉色。
Anselm　我的新公寓。

＊·什麼是你們生活中不能缺少的？
Anselm　Holly。

＊·要不要跟大家分享你們的祕密？
Sam　不要。

＊·要不要跟大家分享你哥哥 / 弟弟的祕密？
Sam　不知道他任何秘密，否則就不會是秘密了。
Anselm　在他小時候——大約七歲時，有一天他放學回家跟媽咪說第二天是個特別的慈善捐款日，可以穿漂亮的衣服去學校，但要付錢好讓學校去做慈善工作。於是我媽整晚沒睡為他做了一整套俠盜羅賓漢的衣服，包括一件綠色緊身衣和一件斗篷。然而事實上第二天根本沒有什麼慈善日，他只是想穿著羅賓漢的衣服去上學而已。其他小孩都穿牛仔褲和T恤。

What keeps you going and stay in tune?
Anselm   Life.

What's your favourite drink, music & film?
Sam   Guinness, Rockabilly, Country, Soul, *The Producers, Some like it Hot* and any Marx Brothers movie.
Anselm   Modello beer/coffe, the cure/pixies/esg/the supremes/ELVIS.

What would be a special treat for you?
Anselm   To see Elvis in concert.

What's your usual way of cooking potato?
Sam   Baked.
Anselm   Chips.

What have you not tried to do, but would definitely want to try one day?
Anselm   Sky diving.

What is your latest obsession?
Sam   Neon pink.
Anselm   My new flat.

What can't you live without?
Anselm   Holly.

Dare to share one of your secrets?
Sam   Nope.

Dare to share one of your brother's secrets?
Sam   Don't know any otherwise they wouldn't be secrets.
Anselm   When he was a little boy, about seven, he came home from school and told our mum that the next day at school was a special charity day. You had to pay to go to school in fancy dress. So my mum stayed up all night making him a Robin Hood outfit complete with green tights and a cloak. However it wasn't really a special day at school he just felt like going to School in a cloak and tights, all the other kids were in jeans and t-shirts.

Chatwin Brothers 的壁紙 / 包裝紙圖騰

我設計的小鳥 noobery，快樂地飛翔在 Noodle town 中，相關資訊請上 www.noodoll.co.uk 查詢

此書完成尾聲，正好也碰上 noodoll 英國商展，是我設計工作特別繁忙的時刻。
每天一睜開眼就是快速跳下床，生活的節奏彷彿以影片快轉速度進行，忙得昏頭轉向。

商展結束之後，準備搭隔天的飛機回台灣，卻在倫敦機場辦理登機手續時，
一不留神讓我的寶貝手提電腦被偷了:(
我的作品，我的心血，我的所有重要資料，以及太多太多一忙就忘了備份的東西全都在裡面，
其中包括這本書20%的內容也這樣飛了⋯⋯

整躺飛行旅程，煎熬，非常氣自己的不小心，當時真的很想乾脆跳機；
也氣這些莫名其妙，heartless，偷人心血的小偷，祝他們倒霉。

事情發生之後，媽媽一直鼓勵我向前看，記住教訓，不要停留在不開心的記憶中。
所以在台灣立刻又買了一台手提電腦，重新出發。
心痛很多丟掉的東西永遠找不回來，像我為這本書拍攝的很多市集和人物照片，
和這幾年來數不清的 noodoll 來自世界各地朋友的 email lists。

將這件事寫出來是因為它成了這本書曲折完成的一個重要過程，
非常謝謝我的朋友 Sean* 立刻又去倫敦市集幫我補拍了一些照片，
所以大家看到本書一開始的市集照片都是他大力協助之下的成果。

也謝謝 John，媽媽，爸爸 及 Leon, Chris, 嘟嘟貝貝武爸武媽，
曲姐家林曲爸曲媽，Alice 王伯王阿姨，在得知這件事情後的第一時間關心和幫助。

* Sean Lee，在我的第一本創意市集中介紹過
http://www.horaceandthesailingzebra.com

國立中央圖書館出版品預行編目資料

創意市集 II - 玩心大發 Fashion Market II -
Interviews with 13 UK artists/designers from the
fashion market / 王怡穎 作 --初版--臺北市；田園
城市文化事業有限公司，民94(2005)
　　　　　　面；　　　　公分
　　　　　　ISBN 986-7705-85-8（平裝）
1. 工業設計

962　　　　　　　　　94012983

創意市集II
玩心大發

作者　　　王怡穎 (Yi-Ying Wang)
ISBN　　　986-7705-85-8
譯者　　　黃心心
藝術編輯　林銀玲
企畫編輯　席　芬
發行人　　陳炳槮
發行所　　田園城市文化事業有限公司
地址　　　104 台北市中山北路二段72巷6號
電話　　　(02)25319081
傳真　　　(02)25319085
定價　　　300 元
登記證　　新聞局局版台業字第6314號
郵政劃撥　19091744
戶名　　　田園城市文化事業有限公司
初版一刷　西元 2005 年 9 月
初版六刷　西元 2007 年 4 月
網址　　　www.gardencity.com.tw
電子信箱　gardenct@ms14.hinet.net
版權所有‧翻印必究

All rights reserved. No part of this publication
may be reproduced.

The artworks, images, products, trademarks
and logos used in this book are copyrighted
or otherwise protected by legislation and
cannot be reproduced without the permission
of the holder of the rights.